THE HUNGER FOR SIGNIFICANCE

FOREWORD BY CHARLES COLSON

R.C. SPROUL

THE HUNGER FOR SIGNIFICANCE

Regal Books

A Division of GL Publications
Ventura, California, U.S.A.

Published by Regal Books
A Division of Gospel Light
Ventura, California, U.S.A.
Printed in U.S.A.

Regal Books is a ministry of Gospel Light, an evangelical Christian publisher dedicated to serving the local church. We believe God's vision for Gospel Light is to provide church leaders with biblical, user-friendly materials that will help them evangelize, disciple and minister to children, youth and families.

It is our prayer that this Regal Book will help you discover biblical truth for your own life and help you meet the needs of others. May God richly bless you.

For a free catalog of resources from Regal Books/Gospel Light please contact your Christian supplier or call 1-800-4-GOSPEL.

Scripture quotations, unless otherwise indicated, are the author's own translation. Versions quoted include:

KJV—*King James Version.*

NIV—Scripture quotations marked *(NIV)* are from the HOLY BIBLE, NEW INTERNATIONAL VERSION. Copyright © 1973, 1978, 1984 International Bible Society. Used by permission of Zondervan Bible Publishers.

RSV—From *RSV* of the Bible, copyrighted 1946 and 1952 by the Division of Christian Education of the NCCC, U.S.A., and used by permission.

Formerly published under the title *In Search of Dignity.*

Any omission of credits is unintentional. The publisher requests documentation for future printings.

Library of Congress Cataloging-in-Publication Data
Sproul, R.C. (Robert Charles), 1939-
    The hunger for significance / R.C. Sproul
        p.   cm.
    Rev. ed. of: In search of dignity. c1983.
    Includes bibliographical references.
    ISBN 0-8307-1687-4 (trade)
    1. Dignity—Religious aspects—Christianity. I. Sproul, R.C. (Robert Charles), 1939-
In search of dignity. II. Title.
BV4647.D5S67   1991   91-27918
241'.4—dc20   CIP

1 2 3 4 5 6 7 8 9 10 11 12 / X3.2 / KP / 01 00 99 98 97 96 95 94

Rights for publishing this book in other languages are contracted by Gospel Literature International (GLINT). GLINT also provides technical help for the adaptation, translation, and publishing of Bible study resources and books in scores of languages worldwide. For further information, contact GLINT, Post Office Box 4060, Ontario, California, 91761-1003, U.S.A., or the publisher.

To James McIntyre, who bestowed upon me
the priceless gift of dignity,
and
to my comrades on the staff
of Ligonier Ministries.

CONTENTS

FOREWORD

SOME years ago a friend suggested I watch a lecture on videocassette by a theologian named R.C. Sproul. I wasn't particularly excited about the prospect.

I had heard Sproul's name once or twice and knew little about him except that he was a theologian. That wasn't an especially appealing qualification since I was an activist, working every day in the battlefields of human need; theology was for people who had time to study. Besides, I thought, theologians lived in thick-walled ivory towers and wouldn't be able to speak practically enough for me.

But, at my friend's urging, I agreed to watch Sproul's series on the holiness of God. That decision led to one of the most remarkable experiences of my Christian life—at the end of the sixth lecture I found myself prostrate, awed and begging for God's mercy. Through Sproul's remarkable gift of communication, I came to know God that day in a profound way I had not known Him before.

Shortly thereafter I visited R.C. Sproul at the Ligonier Ministries; we spent a weekend discussing some particularly tough questions about the Christian faith. Those three days were marvelously fulfilling.

In my varied career in business, law, government and in evangelical circles, I have been exposed to some of the great minds of the twentieth century. That weekend I realized that R.C. ranks among the top five or six intellects I have known. I have studied under his tutelage ever since.

That was also the beginning of a friendship that I have come to treasure greatly, one which has inspired me, taught me, challenged me and encouraged me.

What is remarkable about R.C. is that while he is respected as one of the keenest Christian apologists and theologians in the world today, he has the extraordinary capacity to communicate profound truth in a very simple way. He is no ivory tower scholar. Rather, he is a thinker who communicates to people where they are—in the work place, the pew, the home, the prison.

That is why this book is so powerful. It speaks in understandable terms to one of the most critical issues of our day—the dignity and worth of man.

Look at our modern civilization. Machines are replacing people. Incredible technological progress in our century has taken authority away from the individual and vested it in huge impersonal institutions.

And people often don't care. For many, reality is no longer their own lives, but what they see transmitted in living color across the electronic screen in their living room night after night.

The twentieth-century technocracy has left man feeling helpless, alienated and impotent. At the same time, forces of humanism have been on the rise, telling us that man has no ultimate purpose beyond living for the moment. What we do, indeed, who we are, has no absolute meaning.

So why not do whatever one wants—or nothing? If life is without meaning, so is the individual.

That loss of meaning, purpose and individual dignity is the growing malaise of our times. The only sane response can be the Christian worldview that reveals we are created in the image of

God, that our souls are eternal while empires will fall and machines rust away.

As Christians, we see full well the overwhelming spiritual bankruptcy of our society—but the real question is, what do we *do* about it?

This book gives those answers, applying biblical perspectives on worth and value to the home, the workplace, the church, the hospital, the prison. In doing so, R.C. Sproul has sounded a call for our times; he has joined the battle between humanist myth and Christian dignity.

I hope as you read this revealing book you'll come to know R.C. Sproul, and that he may do for you what he did for me— drive you to your knees in awe of the holy God.

For it is our God who will lift you up and take you out onto the streets, meeting people at the point of need with a message that ought to be shouted from the rooftops by every Christian:

> "Life is not meaningless, man is not without worth! Our Christ died on the cross that we might be with Him eternally. God made us for a purpose. We must see ourselves—and one another—in light of the dignity He gives us."

That is good news, especially as our society discovers that when it believes in everything it really believes in nothing. This book equips the believer in the living God with magnificent insights and answers for a world desperately yearning for meaning.

Charles W. Colson
Washington, D.C.

PREFACE

A search can be fun—from hide-and-seek to hunting Easter eggs on the White House lawn; from looking for a hot spot where the fish are biting to the scavenger hunt at a Halloween party.

A search can be futile—from the ancient Diogenes examining the darkest corners of Athens with his lantern, looking in vain for an honest man, to the medieval knight pursuing the Holy Grail; from the quest for the Lost Dutchman mine to the lure of discovering Shangri-la.

A search can be tedious, yielding its reward after countless hours and lingering years of failure—Thomas Edison experimenting with a thousand substances before finding one suitable for use as a glowing filament; Jonas Salk peering through a thousand microscopes before finding a vaccine for polio.

A search can be quixotic—the alchemist seeking a formula to turn lead into gold; Ponce De León tracking down the Fountain of Youth. It is searching for gold at the end of the rainbow and chasing the will-o'-the-wisp with a butterfly net.

A search can be maniacal—Captain Ahab sailing his troubled soul into uncharted waters, risking his crew and his mission to gain revenge on his loathsome nemesis, the great white whale Moby Dick. It is the giant in Jack and the Beanstalk shouting, "Fee fi fo fum" while frantically chasing after his golden harp.

Man is by nature a hunter. He longs to discover the new

frontier, the lost horizon, the magic formula and the ultimate tro-
phy. From Nimrod stalking the primordial lion to Nazi-hunter
Simon Wiesenthal's relentless pursuit of Adolf Eichmann and
Dr. Josef Mengele, the hunt is fierce. It is Columbus seeking a
new world, Galileo a new moon around Jupiter, and Christian
Dior a new flair for fashion.

We are the seekers. We hunt for animals and precious gems;
for a cure for cancer and a way to solve the national debt. We
look for jobs, for dates, for bargains and for thrills. The pursuit
of happiness is our inalienable right. We are like Dorothy, off to
see the Wizard, the wonderful Wizard of Oz.

Ours is a new world, fraught with the peril of nuclear annihilation, torn by the violence of international terrorism, embittered by our failure to build the great society. The rigorous pursuit of our day is the search for dignity and personal worth. It
is a mighty quest fueled by the flames of passion that burn in the
souls of people who refuse to surrender to the voices which
declare we are nothing.

The search for dignity is a titanic struggle, an epic adventure,
prodded by a pain that will not go away. Modern man has an
aching void. The emptiness we feel cannot be relieved by one
more gourmet meal or another snort of cocaine. We carry water
in a sieve when we try to fill the empty space with a better job
or a bigger house.

Dignity is never found in plastic. We must search further
and probe deeper if the haunting cries of indignity are to be
silenced. Ours must be a transcendent quest—going beyond the
trivial to the ultimate questions of our worth as human beings.

It was Saint Augustine who declared that within each of us
is a vacuum which must be filled if the rape of insignificance is
to miss us in its vicious attack. We must seek our roots, our origin, and our destiny if we are to know our present value.

This book is written by a Christian for Christians and for
anyone else who shares in the search. It explores the human cry

for dignity, the deep desire for significance, the hallowed longing for love and respect. It touches the aching void in the home, the school, the hospital, the prison, the church and the workplace. Wherever people come together, hunters meet in common cause—the discovery of worth, the assurance of our dignity.

At times the book is autobiographical—not as if I alone have felt the aching void but that I may speak from the most intimate chamber of my quest, my own heart. Some will identify and others will not. My pain is not always your pain. And my delight may leave you bored.

But my earnest hope is that at some point our kindred spirits will meet, and whatever else óur differences, we will be cemented together in a renewed commitment to preserve and protect the dignity of the men, women and children who surround us every day.

My gratitude must be expressed to Bob and Lillian Love for providing me with a place to work, far from the intrusions of ringing phones and administrative pressures, and to Leo and Todge Collins for helping me with support material. Special thanks go to Mrs. Lillian Rowe for allowing the tender moments of her husband's death to be included in the book.

Thanks also to Karen Snellback for typing the manuscript, to Tim Couch and Dave Fox for running the ship of the Ligonier Ministries in my absence, to my son R. C. Sproul, Jr. for editorial assistance, and to my friends at Regal Books: William Greig, David Malme, and my patient editor Donald Pugh for prodding me to write the book, and for all their encouragement and assistance.

Finally, my heartfelt thanks to my wife, Vesta, without whose help this book would be far more abstract and far less readable.

R.C. Sproul
Altamonte Springs, Florida
July 1991

CHAPTER ONE OUR SEARCH FOR PERSONAL WORTH

THE shrill blast of the whistle reverberated from the cold walls of the gymnasium. All action ceased instantly as boys froze in position, halting in midstride as if playing the childhood game of statues. Every eye turned to Mac who was standing in front of the bench, his face crimson from rage and the paroxysm of fury unleashed in the whistle blast. He stood in the menacing position of a policeman who has just caught wayward youths in an act of vandalism: hands on hips, legs spread apart, chin jutting aggressively, signaling a dare for anyone to make a false move.

Mac was not just a coach—he was *the* coach, commanding all the blend of fear and respect the platoon sergeant engenders in raw recruits. His face was angular with high granite cheekbones, sharp chin, and eyes deeply recessed within bony sockets. His hair was red, not the carrot color associated with the Campbell's Soups boy, but the more mature type, splashed with a sandy tint. At the moment, picking up the hue radiating from his face, his hair appeared vermilion as if flames were bursting from the crown of his head

The whistle dropped from his lips, bobbing from the chain around his neck. A sardonic grin spread slowly across his face as he spoke softly but powerfully: "Well, what have we here? A prima donna?"

The smile evaporated and through clenched teeth he shouted my name, "Sproul! Take a walk. Hit the showers. You're done for today."

I was standing 20 feet from the locker room but the distance seemed infinite, as if my feet would have to carry me across an unbridgeable chasm to safety. I buried my chin in my chest, trying desperately to lift my shoulders high enough to conceal my blushing face as I began to slink toward the sanctuary of the locker room. Every eye was riveted on me as I made my exit, feeling the disgrace and shame of the cadet forced to march the parade of dishonor before his peers.

The seemingly interminable walk finally ended as the door swung shut behind me and the rhythmic bouncing of basketballs thumping against the hardwood floors started up again. I exhaled a deep sigh as I sat down on the bench in front of my locker and began peeling off my uniform and unraveling the tape from my ankles. The room seemed eerie to me, sitting there alone, without the usual banter and playful jostling that was part of the daily ritual of suiting up. The silence was dreadful; I could hear my every breath echoing from the steel lockers and tiled walls.

My feeling of isolation grew more intense as I stepped into the spacious shower stall, built to accommodate 12 boys at a time, each with his own shower nozzle and soap dish. As the sharp spray of hot water pounded my shoulders I was feeling the sting of the coach's words.

What had I done to deserve expulsion? I was not guilty of a temper tantrum or sassing the coach. I had merely engaged in a little bit of harmless clowning around.

Practice began each day with a routine passing drill which involved groups of boys moving from one end of the court to the other by passes alone. No dribbles were allowed, no steps could be taken, as the drill was designed to sharpen the skill of dexterous ball handling. For some of the players the drill was excruciating, revealing tendencies toward clumsiness.

But my hero was Marquis Haynes, the dribble-wizard of the Harlem Globetrotters, and I had spent hours in my own backyard court practicing moves far more advanced than this elementary exercise. What could be the harm in showing off? Besides, I was the team captain and the star, which should entitle me to the privileges of status.

So on this day, instead of going through the paces of the normal routine, I dressed it up a little with stutter steps to make the rhythm more complex, and behind the back passes to my comrades, moving up the floor culminating with the *piece de resistance*, the *coup de grace*, a shot I had perfected in my backyard, which was a new invention. I held the ball completely behind my back and, with a hard flick of my wrist with neck bent forward, I flipped the ball over my head toward the basket.

The play was a thing of beauty to behold and I carried it off adroitly, moving down the floor in graceful fluidity, not missing a beat, executing my magic shot with a perfect swish. That was when the whistle blasted me out of my glory.

I quit the shower and dressed quickly, slipping out a backdoor of the school, hoping no one would see me leave. It was snowing and instead of savoring the five-mile ride home in Mac's car, I had to walk. The road ribboned through rural countryside before it entered the suburb where I lived. I tramped through the snow, oblivious to the surroundings as two words kept attacking my brain over and over again, "prima donna, prima donna, prima donna...."

Twenty years later a friend jokingly called me a prima donna and was flabbergasted by my reaction to the words. I hate them with a passion, as they are encased in my fragile psyche with a special toxic power to them. Those words are loaded for me in a way which makes them loathsome.

Words can be like that. I was once in a conversation which included Charles Colson, the warm, deeply committed Christian who founded Prison Fellowship International. Before he became a Christian, Colson had served as counsel to President Nixon and went to prison for his role in the Watergate scandal.

During the conversation, someone remarked, "You're beating a dead horse." Instantly Colson's countenance changed; his eyes glazed over and his face froze in pain. Though seemingly innocent, the remark was far too loaded for him to bear.

When Colson faced prison during the Watergate trials, his defense attorney was abruptly interrupted in the midst of his pleas before the bench by the stern words of the judge, "Hold it, counselor, you're beating a dead horse." With those words, Colson was sentenced to prison and the otherwise innocuous expression was branded in his mind forever.

Similarly, with the words *prima donna* I was humiliated, cut down from my pride. I was guilty as charged and I knew it, making the words all the more painful for me.

I wanted to be a good basketball player. I wanted to be a great basketball player. I never made it.

What was worse is that on that day I broke the athlete's code of humility and played the glory-hound, the show-off, the hotdog. That type of antic is readily acceptable now with the patented dunk shots of basketball players and carefully choreographed touchdown rituals of the National Football League; but in the '50s such displays were anathema, communicating an intolerable lack of sportsmanship.

OUR ASPIRATION FOR SIGNIFICANCE

Why do we do such things?

Deeply ensconced in the marrow of our bones is the *aspi-*

ration for significance. The phrase is abstract but it defines the clamoring beat of every human heart for self-esteem.

Why We Want Our Lives to Count

We want our lives to count. We yearn to believe that in some way we are important. This inner drive is as intense as our need for water and oxygen.

We argue about religion and politics, abortion and homosexuality, nuclear weapons and welfare programs. We bicker about a host of things, but at one point we are all in harmony: every person among us wants to be treated with dignity and worth.

The hunger for esteem is the propelling force behind the entrepreneur's brilliant enterprise, the athlete's competitive spirit, the warrior's lust for conquest. This elemental drive has been dissected and analyzed by scholars, peeled layer by layer and subjected to the closest scrutiny, only to be praised by some and damned by others. No sentient person, however, denies the brute fact of this drive in all of us.

The aspiration for significance can be known by other names and called by other terms. The businessman might call it "success motivation" or the "goal of achievement." Our founding fathers spoke of it as the "pursuit of happiness."

The hunger for significance is consuming, and when it eludes us it leaves an empty void gnawing to be filled. The hollow point aches for satisfaction. We dream, we hope, we fantasize our moment in the sun, hoarding the scraps of success in the trophy room of our souls.

More often we fail. We lose. We come in second.

We fix tomorrow as the due date for success but tomorrow becomes today and the magic moment is postponed. Some adjust their goals, others surrender to despair, still others go mad. It is Willie Loman's losing touch with reality, dreaming of the ultimate shoe sale; it is Archie Bunker using prejudice *to*

assure himself he did not finish last; it is John McEnroe throwing a temper tantrum at Wimbledon; it is pro baseball's late
Billy Martin kicking dirt on an umpire.

Some are driven to try harder, reaching down into a hidden
reservoir of strength, finding new sources of energy to muffle the
inner voices that accuse them. We cannot bear to lose. We weep
for ourselves, sometimes with quiet dignity, other times with
inarticulate moans and sometimes with piercing screams. We
make excuses, point at others for cheating us and march in
protest with picket signs.

Why would women enter coal mines and risk their lives in
subterranean caverns or climb in police cruisers to brave the
felons' guns? Why would Janet Guthrie drive a race car in the
Indianapolis 500? Why would Ann Richards take on the job of
governor of Texas or Sandra O'Connor don the robes of a
supreme court justice?

Why?

For the same reason men do it, to strive for significance.
The quest for significance crosses sexual lines. It is a human quest
that involves every man and every woman.

Consider Max Anderson and Ben Abruzzo, who ventured
to be the first human beings to cross the Atlantic Ocean in a heli-
um-filled balloon after all previous attempts had failed with the
loss of five lives. Their first attempt in *Double Eagle* aborted in
the frigid waters of Iceland, leaving Ben Abruzzo permanently
crippled from severe frostbite and his body weakened by
hypothermia. Why in 1978 would the two men, both millionaires
in their own right, try it again and succeed in *Double Eagle II*?

Charles McCarry answers that question in his chronicle of the
event.

> It was possible to die. But if you did, you would first
> have lived through the worst things a man can face:
> storms at great altitudes, wind, rain, snow, ice, light-

ning—uncontrollable and unimaginable forces. You would go in one side of the unknown in an open gondola, suspended beneath a bag filled with gas so slippery, so thin, that it could pour through a mere pinhole in the fabric, hemorrhaging helium as a pierced heart spurts blood. If you had the skill and the nerve, and the Spartan discipline, to come out the other side alive, you would be a man unlike any other.[1]

Our search for personal worth has been described in a vari-

Multitudes of people take their pay level as a barometer to record their personal worth as persons.

---

ety of ways. The metaphor of the "pyramid principle" is used to describe the structure of society. Like the pyramid, society has a broad base with much room at the bottom.

From the base, society moves upward, not in parallel lines to form a square, but in lines which converge at the peak of the pyramid. Each level of the pyramid has a rank, a social echelon marked in ascending fashion moving toward the apex. There is but the tiniest space at the top and few can attain it. Yet people fight to move away from the masses buried at the bottom, seeking the higher esteem associated with the top levels.

We want to hold our index finger in the air, shouting, "We are number one!" We want to win the race of rats and move up the organizational ladder.

The principle of upward mobility defines the mad dash of the social climber and the importance of the "register" to the elitist.

The right schools, the proper attire, the finely honed etiquette—all attest to one's niche on the pyramid.

The world has been saturated with blood by madmen scrambling for the top. The desire to get ahead, to move up, can incite the worst degrees of selfishness and cruelest forms of ruthlessness within us. The evil that flows from the quest can make our desire for significance nothing more than an animal-like lust to dominate.

We must pause for a moment of caution lest we throw the baby out with the bathwater. Our quest for esteem can take on a Jekyll-Hyde character; our virtues can become vices if not tempered by restraint. The quest for worth can become a lust for power; the desire for significance can make us egomaniacs, blind to everything but our own success.

When Our Goals Collide
The problem is people. I am a person and I seek to be respected by other people. Those other people also want to be respected, and sometimes their goals and mine collide.

What happens when our goals collide determines how we value people. We can treat our differences in a spirit of mutual respect or seek to crush each other with brutality.

The search for significance is not wicked in itself; no evil dwells in the desire for achievement. To improve our performance adds to self-esteem while making us more productive in the process. But if our climb is over the dead and mutilated bodies of other people, then the aspiration for significance has run amuck.

There is a thin line between wickedness and nobility. The seven deadly sins are but seven created aspirations gone askew. They are seven blessed virtues become seven deadly distortions.

Self-esteem corrupts to *pride*; the quest for material welfare crosses the border to *covetousness*; the hunger for personal intimacy degenerates to *lust.* Pain turns to *anger* and hunger to *gluttony.* Admiration and honor are sullied by *envy,* and our need for rest surrenders to *sloth.*

What is it that makes us people and not mere animals? We speak of the rat race as if we were brutish rodents rushing about a maze, seeking the passage that will lead to one more bit of cheese. Sometimes we behave as beasts, but every fiber of our bodies protests that we are not dumb animals and we resent it when others treat us as if we were.

When We Are Treated Beneath Our Dignity

It hurts when we are treated beneath our dignity. We have unwritten rules which define our social status. Even in high school, a clear pecking order was established. The educational curriculum, like Gaul, was divided into three parts: College Preparatory, General, and Vocational, ranked socially in that order.

Graduation brought other subtle distinctions to the surface. At the top of the social list were those enrolled in college, followed in order by nurses school, business or secretarial school, vocational school, the armed forces, and finally by those who were finished with formal education and opted for jobs.

I prided myself on my lack of snobbishness about going to college, where I found another structure of social prestige divided between the various academic majors. I endorsed the all-men-are-created-equal creed and despised the middle-class addiction to status symbols. Then something happened which caught me in the embarrassing discovery that I was lying to myself.

I was a philosophy major and proud of it, seeing the discipline as the domain of the intellectual elite. But summer vacation posed a problem. The want ads listed few requests for part-time neophyte philosophers.

While my friends from the science department landed lucrative summer jobs as laboratory assistants, I was looking for ditches to dig where I could cogitate between shovel loads. I spent one summer digging graves, and the next I was a laborer at a city hospital.

One summer morning as I was sweeping up cigarette butts and other debris from the front steps of the hospital, I noticed a group of nursing students approaching the entrance. I leaned on my broom, flashed my most charming smile and said, "Good morning."

No response. They passed me by as though I were a miserable beggar too lowly to be acknowledged.

I had to stifle the impulse to run after them, shouting, "Hey, wait. You don't understand. I'm not really a laborer. I'm a college guy—a philosophy major and everything!"

I identified for a moment with John H. Griffin, the investigative reporter who had written a series of articles and then a book about the indignities he experienced while posing as a black man in a white man's world.

The snub by the student nurses did not go unnoticed. Another laborer, the janitor in charge of the nurses school across the street, observed my obvious discomfort. He crossed the street and warmly introduced himself, speaking with a thick foreign accent.

When I explained to him that I was a college student studying philosophy he started asking me pointed questions about heavy philosophical matters. I felt silly talking philosophy to a janitor who could hardly speak English. I was soon astonished, however, by his obvious mastery of the subject and started asking questions of him.

His story overwhelmed me as he explained that he was a survivor of Dachau, one of Hitler's infamous death camps. He had been arrested and sent to the concentration camp only weeks before he was due to complete his doctorate in philosophy in a German university. His views had attracted the interest of the Gestapo, the dreaded Nazi secret police organization.

His wife and three of his children died in the gas chambers of Dachau. He and one daughter survived. Since coming to this country, he had labored continuously with one consuming passion: to get his daughter through school. He swelled with pride as he told me she had just graduated from the University of Pittsburgh a few weeks earlier.

I went back to my broom and the cigarette butts, profoundly ashamed of my own tale of the woes of indignity, wondering if I had just met an angel unawares.

How We Measure Our Self-worth
We tend to measure our self-worth by how our work is valued. Salary levels and pay scales mean more to us than the material goods money will buy. Whether it is appropriate or not, multitudes of people take their pay level as a barometer to record their worth as persons.

In a society where such terms of human value are considered, a burden of doubt is cast upon the person at the lower end of the pay-scale mechanism. A shadow falls across the brightness of his own image, making him feel the sting of the question of whether his life is worthless.

Socrates declared, "The unexamined life is not worth living." True, few of the laboring class reach the Socratic level of self-examination, but the message of society gets through to the unlettered and uncultured just the same. Formal education is not needed for one to comprehend the judgment, "You really are not worth very much."

Yet, the man labors on, hoping against hope that the judgment of society is at least partially wrong. *Some day*, he thinks, *people will recognize that I have value.*

In the meantime he seeks his affirmation from his wife and children and, if that fails, from his dog. Dogs tend to be totally ignorant of the protocol of status.

Beyond the home exists the camaraderie of the tavern, the vicarious thrill of the victories of his favorite sports team, the secret hope that he will hit it big in the numbers or win the lottery sweepstakes. Then, he thinks, he will be somebody. Others try to silence the accusing voices with too many boiler-makers or to seek solace by conjuring up a tough-guy image.

When We Intimidate and Dominate to Fulfill Our Aspirations

The tough-guy image, the macho syndrome, is a breeding ground for the bully. "There is always one in the crowd." Every large group has someone in it who adopts the style of the bully in an attempt to wrest a position of leadership and power.

The techniques of the bully may include physical coercion, intellectual intimidation or political extortion. The tactics vary, but the mood is the same. The bully may be successful for a season, but he attains his status with the sacrifice of love and friendship, incurring the contempt of his wounded victims.

The message of the bully is simple: "If you will not love me you will at least respect me. If you do not respect me, you will at least fear me."

A depressing book which became a best-seller was *Winning Through Intimidation.* The author adopts a cynical world-view and gives a handbook on power tactics for succeeding in business. He adopts a twisted version of the Golden Rule for a motto, "Do unto others before they do it unto you."

The world is a highly competitive arena where weakness is rarely an asset. Where competition abounds, intimidation does more abound, as an edge is gained when an opponent is caught in the grip of fear. A frightened enemy is already half-beaten, as every athlete will attest. The tactics of intimidation may be seen in the growling of a linebacker, the stare of the boxer at the weigh-in, the message pitch of the brush-back artist and the high-flying stick of the "enforcer" on the hockey rink.

Sam Snead, a threetime Masters champion, relates that in the golden era of match play on the golf circuit, he became more aggressive the moment he noticed the glint of fear in his opponent's eyes or the change in tempo of his opponent's rhythm of smoking. These were telltale signs of an inner tightening that is customarily described as "choking." Since fear is so paralyzing a force, it is not strange that the intense competitor will seek to instill it in his opponent.

If the Lombardiism of "winning isn't everything, it is the only thing" is true, then ethics have no place in the realm of competition. But Vince Lombardi did not believe the clever saying

---

Competition provides the zest for our aspirations, but the zest is burdened by the...lust for dominance.

---

that is so often attributed to him.[2] His impeccable record as a coach would not have earned him the accolades he received had his victories been sullied by unsportsmanlike conduct.

It does matter how you play the game, and the public soon tires of the antics of the athletic bully or the spoiled brats of professional sports whose tantrums violate the spirit of the games. The villains of the old video days of studio wrestling were carefully choreographed to lose, as the promoters understood that the public delights in seeing the bully vanquished. We root for the underdog, joining the plea of Adrian, "Win, Rocky."

The line between the intense competitor and the tyrant is thin. It is the line that separates beauty and ugliness. It is the line between Jack Nicklaus and Jack the Ripper, between Queen Elizabeth and Lizzie Borden.

The tyrant's stock and trade is fear. Without fear he cannot rule. To stay in power, the totalitarian government depends on keeping the populace in fear. The pogrom, the secret police, the bloody purge and the art of extortion are the weapons of the tyrant. These are the politics of intimidation, and they find their less sophisticated counterparts on the floor of every factory, in the cloakrooms of every corporation and in the sexual harassment of the business office.

Competition provides the zest for our aspirations, but the zest is burdened by the ease with which our nobility suffers from the fatal flaw of ruthless lust for dominance. Too little drive for significance yields personal inertia; too much breeds tyranny.

As evil reveals the brilliant glory of virtue, so tyranny and ruthless competition accent the reality of our innate need for significance. Let the instinct wither and life becomes paltry; let the instinct run rampant without restraint and life becomes cruel.

THE SEARCH FOR RESPECT

Only in America can a man earn a million dollars by telling one joke. The joke is cast in a wide variety of backdrops and life situations, but the punch line remains forever the same. Comedian Rodney Dangerfield makes his living with the same line repeated incessantly: "I get no respect."

Why We Laugh at Disrespect

What is it that makes it possible for us to laugh at the dismal plight of a man who gets no respect? Are we a nation of masochists who enjoy a vicarious pleasure from suffering the pain of indignity? Or are we a nation of sadists who get our pleasure from reducing another person to abject humiliation?

Perhaps our laughter springs from a different source, being akin to the emotions that make it seem appropriate to whistle in the dark. Perhaps we laugh because we cannot afford to cry.

I remember a sugar maple tree that marked the outer edge of an apple orchard which had survived the bulldozers of a new suburban development. The orchard was a geographical anomaly standing as a buffer zone between our tree-lined street and the community shopping center.

As a boy, I loved to walk through the orchard on my way to the store—except at night, and especially in the winter, as the boughs of that great maple were bare of leaves and stretched their grotesque tentacles into the night. When the moon was bright, I could look up from the center of the orchard and see the frightening arms of the tree looming in front of me like some giant bogeyman about to grab me. I used to experience stark terror as I walked past the tree.

My custom was to whistle softly as I passed by, stuffing my hands in my pockets and assuming a casual gait as I sauntered by my nemesis. My whistling was soft because fear had taken any surplus breath from me. What a strange thing to do, as if the tree could be deceived by my outward display of cavalier courage.

So we laugh at disrespect as if by so doing we can fool its power, hoping it will not reach out and make us its next victim.

No one likes to be insulted or to be made fun of. The one who is the butt of other people's fun is left outside the camp of humor. To lose respect is to be crushed in the inner spirit; it is to be humiliated.

How Compliments Enhance Our Dignity

Conversely, it is affirming to be praised and honored by other people. Such honors may be embarrassing at times, particularly if a shy person is thrust too swiftly into the center of attention, but generally we prefer the compliment to the insult, as the compliment enhances our dignity while the insult demeans it.

The organization which employs me once engaged the professional services of a management consultant. I looked forward to spending time with him to discover insights about management structures, models and the like. My first encounter turned out to be a surprise as he devoted his attention to probing my personality and emotional makeup before we could get down to business.

His opening gambit was to raise the following question: "What are the five most meaningful compliments you've ever received?"

The consultant handed me a pencil and a piece of paper and asked me to jot down in brief the five compliments that came to my mind, noting from whom I had received them and at what point in my life they had come. I filled out the paper as instructed and was surprised by the things I discovered about myself and my life.

One of the five memorable compliments I wrote on the paper came from my eighth-grade English teacher after completing a homework assignment. We had been instructed to write a descriptive paragraph, letting our imaginations roam freely as we made our virgin attempt at creative writing. When the papers were graded the teacher announced, "Before I return these papers, there is one I want to read aloud."

To my unmitigated shock, she exposed to the ears of everyone in the class the content of my descriptive paragraph and posted my paper on the bulletin board where everyone could see it. Few grasped the significance of that act for my dignity. The bulletin board was normally reserved for the display of the students' artwork. I was the poorest art student in the class and had the ignominious distinction of being the only student to never have had his artwork displayed on the bulletin board.

In one fell swoop, I made the big time as my English composition was considered a work of art. After class, I went to the front of the room to gaze at the impossible, to stare at my trophy which carried me to the heights of glory. There, emblazoned on the margin, beneath the grade, were the words of my teacher, "R.C., don't ever let anyone tell you that you can't write."

Do you have any idea how many people have since tried to tell me I cannot write?

Who in his right mind would be foolhardy enough to risk the red pencils of the critics by putting his work into print? Do you realize there are people out there who make money by being professional critics? They are the people who give meaning to the word anxiety for filmmakers, playwrights and authors.

The scourge of the author is to compose a manuscript, submit it to the critical scrutiny of a publisher, only to receive the dreaded reply of rejection. If one is successful enough to get a

---

It is the authentic compliment, sincerely offered, that enhances human dignity and builds a reservoir of encouragement.

---

manuscript accepted in provisional form, that is merely the beginning of the red pencil syndrome.

One of my books went through seven revisions before I submitted the final polished version. At that point, my editor voiced fair warning, saying, "You've never been through our copy-editing procedures. Don't be discouraged if they make numerous critical suggestions."

I assured my kindly editor that I would not be offended by a rigorous process of amendment, as it would afford me a much-needed free course in copy editing. When I received my manuscript back from the copy editor, however, it had so much red ink it looked like the balance sheet of the Chrysler Corporation before Lee Iacocca took over.

I don't know exactly how many marks were on the manuscript, but I made a fair estimate. I counted the number of marks on the first 10 pages and then figured an average for the entire manuscript. The estimate totaled approximately 10,000 critical marks.

That finding should be enough to convince the most recalcitrant egomaniac that he ought to give up. But there they were, the words of my teacher, "Never let anyone tell you that you can't write." And here I am again, writing my fool fingers off.

The Treasured Compliment. After I had listed my "five most meaningful compliments," my management consultant then went on to give me a crash course in the psychology of the well-timed and well-placed compliment. He asserted that we tend to treasure compliments given to us from *people we esteem.* If we respect the person who pays us a compliment, we will be more likely to cherish the praise and nurse it to our bosom. Such praise will add steel to our brittle self-respect.

The compliments that appear on a list of "most meaningful" are those given by people in positions of authority or leadership over us. The comment of the parent, the teacher, the coach or the boss is the one that carries the extra weight.

The Credibility Factor. Another crucial element that weighs heavily in the value of the compliment is the *credibility factor.* For a compliment to be embraced in the way of permanence it must be believable. People exhibit an uncanny ability to distinguish the compliment from its fraudulent counterpart, flattery.

Flattery is really an insult disguised as a compliment. It appears affirming on the surface, but its dishonest motive sabotages its esteem value. Flattery is designed as a tool of manipulation and is stiff-armed by the recipient.

We have an expression that has moved to the rank of the cliche because of its obvious truth: "Flattery will get you nowhere." The expression exposes the hypocritical design of the remark.

We resist flattery because we do not believe it. A genuine compliment, on the other hand, is believable and we leap to embrace it.

People flatter us at times by lauding our genuine virtues, but they do so with ulterior motives that mar the message, and any complimentary value contained is lost in the morass of manipulation. It is the authentic compliment, sincerely offered, that enhances human dignity and builds a reservoir of encouragement from which we draw when our souls become arid.

How Insults Debase Our Self-image

My consultant's paper had a reverse side to it. After I had finished the above experiment he directed me to turn the paper and list the five most painful insults I had ever received. This was an exercise in pain with no pleasure in it.

Just the writing down of remarks made long ago awakened old wounds within me. I asked myself in the process, "I wonder if the people who said these things to me have any idea how painful they have been?"

My next thought was terrifying: "I wonder how many people would number things I've said to them on their lists of painful insults?"

The power of human speech was suddenly awesome to me.

Just as the genuine compliment can be a catalyst for human encouragement and positive character development, so the insult or thoughtless criticism can have a crippling and paralyzing effect. I think of a stunningly beautiful woman who came to me for counseling. In her mid-30s, she had reached a crisis point in her marriage that was pushing her to despair. She confided that she was affected by a form of sexual frigidity which was ruining her relationship with her husband.

As we discussed her marital history, she revealed that she suffered from a debased self-image, centering on her physical appearance. Twisting her handkerchief in anguish, she blurted out that she couldn't enter freely into sex with her husband because she was so ugly. I was wary at this point, as the woman sitting in front of me, if measured by modern numerical standards, would surely be a "10."

Her story harkened me back to my youth when I had to

endure fishing trips from my mother who, after appearing in a dazzling new dress and with her hair artfully coiffed, would say in mock despair, "I look awful."

I was the "fish" who was to respond to the bait on cue with the appropriate compliment, "Oh, no, Mother, you look wonderful."

I was sure this was a *deja vu* experience calling for the same kind of laudatory assurance. I soon discovered that her grief was not a coquette's charade and that she truly did believe she was ugly. On the surface the self-image appeared utterly groundless. When we probed the past, however, the reasons for her feeling of ugliness emerged with clarity.

The feeling stemmed from an incident that violated her adolescence. As a teenager, her body blossomed early, eliciting hungry looks and words of praise from boys admiring her figure. From the neck down, she was a winner.

The problem centered on her face. She was tormented by recurring acne and made homely by an extra-thick-lensed pair of glasses. Added to these barriers to pulchritude were the cumbersome wires attached to her teeth, designed to make straight what nature had made crooked.

Painfully aware of these physical impediments, she was walking across the playground one day when she overheard one of the upperclass boys comment *sotto voce* to his buddies, "She wouldn't be bad if you put a bag over her head."

The words pierced like a dagger, carrying extra force since their author was a young man deemed the most popular in school. The "standard" of good looks had just delivered a judgment from Olympus and the verdict was devastating.

She carried a poem in her wallet throughout her high school years:

> If love is blind
> And lovers can't see,

Why in the world
Doesn't someone love me?

Twenty years later men would look at her and behold no sign of adolescent acne, no evidence of glasses—as the spectacles had long ago given way to contact lenses and the magic of orthodontia had done its work with braces. The ugly duckling had been marvelously transformed into a beautiful swan in everybody's

---

Christians are particularly vulnerable to the unbridled assault of the tongue.

---

eyes but her own. She was still looking for an appropriate bag in which to hide her head.

Mothers usually give good advice, but not always. My initial encounter with the brutality of social discourse came when an older boy in our neighborhood assaulted me with taunting names. I sought the solace of home and mother's apron.

Drying my tears tenderly, she took the opportunity to instill in me some homespun wisdom designed to serve as a shield against such torment. She said, "Son, when people call you nasty names, don't let that get you down. Just say to them, 'Sticks and stones will break my bones, but names will never hurt me.'"

Armed with this dart-quenching platitude, I returned once more to the arena of social interplay. The bully saw me coming and met me with a maelstrom of verbal abuse. I unleashed my psychological weapon and began to sing, "Sticks and stones...."

I was not able to finish the ditty as my words gave way to choking sobs. My shield collapsed under fire.

The reason my mother's panacea failed is elementary—it simply was not true. Names can hurt and the damage they inflict can be more severe than that wrought by sticks and stones.

Hit me with a stick and break my arm, and in six weeks I have recovered from my injury. Hit me in the head with a stone, opening a bloody gash, and a few stitches can repair the wound. But play havoc with my soul with a brutal insult or an insensitive criticism and you scar me for the rest of my life.

When Our Weaknesses Are Criticized

There is a kind of criticism that is duly named "constructive criticism." Such criticism can peel the opaque film from our eyes, removing the cataracts of self-blindness. Constructive criticism is beneficial, but there are few examples of it. Most of what passes for constructive criticism is, in fact, destructive criticism. The actual ratio cannot be plotted but an educated guess would place it around 95 percent.

Destructive Criticism. Many criticisms we receive are about weaknesses we are already painfully aware of, and most such criticisms tend to tear down rather than to build up. When the criticism is prefaced by the words, "I'm only telling you this for your own good," look out. What follows usually is not designed with a view toward your well-being.

We have been taught to accept such criticism with grace when at times it would be better to run for our lives. When you or I seek to mollify a verbal attack by words of self-defense, the explanation provokes the adversary's further rebuke, "Now don't get defensive."

The perpetrator of verbal abuse not only wants the right to assault you, but demands the further right to do it unimpeded by your natural defense mechanisms. For our critics to presume such rights of assault would be like Joe Montana lining up the San Francisco 49ers for an offensive play only to call time out and protest to the referee that the opposing team was being unfair in placing a defensive unit on the field.

Christians are particularly vulnerable to the unbridled assault of the tongue. We are taught that sanctification requires the practice of humility and a spirit of long-suffering patience. Those virtues are holy indeed, but there is a vast difference between meekness and voluntary doormatism.

Religious persons also may be guilty of abusing the biblical mandate to exhortation and admonishment as a subterfuge for imposing harmful criticism. Be wary of the spiritual "brother" who prefaces his comments with "I want to say something to you in love...." Often what is said in the name of love is a travesty of love.

Authentic constructive criticism may be genuinely offered in love. And its value is inestimable. The point is we must be careful to discern between the constructive and the destructive varieties.

When someone plunges a knife into our soul, it is not our Christian duty to say, "Thank you, dear brother, I needed that. Please push the blade in deeper and twist it a little. It is doing spiritual wonders for me."

The inflicting of thoughtless criticism or the demeaning insult is not only destructive but foolish as well. Little of a positive nature can be gained by it. Even the novice dog trainer knows you cannot improve the animal's obedience by calling the dog "stupid." Yet, we call not only our animals dumb, we use the same kind of disrespectful language for human beings.

I know a highly successful businessman who confesses that the drive in his life was initiated by an irate comment from his mother, "You will never amount to anything." This poor man is driven to prove his mother wrong and takes little satisfaction from his accomplishments as he lives in mortal fear that if he relaxes for a moment, his mother's negative verdict will be proven correct.

Martin Luther King, Jr. once shocked a television talk show host who sought to ruffle King by asking him a racially provocative question, "Dr. King, is it true that black people are lazy, oversexed, and have rhythm?"

King replied coolly, "Quite often it is."

The white interviewer raised his eyebrows at the response.

King went on to qualify his answer. "What do you expect after 200 years of white propaganda? You have been telling the black man for two centuries that he is lazy, oversexed and has rhythm."

The point King was making was that if you impose negative qualities on people long enough, some of the people will begin to act them out because it is clear that you expect them to.

Constructive Criticism. During a seminar with recently graduated registered nurses, we discussed the subject of criticism. During the conversation, one senior supervisor's name was frequently mentioned. The nurses were unsparing in their accolades for that woman's style of giving constructive criticism.

As we inquired about her style, the nurses revealed her secret. At the end of every working day she met privately with each nurse under her charge and asked the same three questions.

She first asked, "What was the most gratifying thing you accomplished today?" The student nurse was encouraged to begin her evaluation period by discussing her daily successes, bringing them to the attention of the supervisor.

The second question was, "What did you do today that you would do differently if you had another opportunity?" This allowed the student to practice self-criticism, which is easier on the ego than listening to the critical evaluation of someone else.

The final question was, "In what areas of your work can I give you help?"

The discussion of the three questions was all that was usually necessary to keep the students on target and in a growing mode. Some tried to invent successes and deny failures, but the supervisor was sharp enough to detect that and put a stop to it. The system worked admirably, producing sound results. Her students felt that she was on their team and were encouraged to greater efforts toward excellence.

The biblical concern for respect is built on the concept of

"honor." The mandate is given repeatedly that we are to "honor one another" (Rom. 12:10, *NIV*). We are called to "honor the king" (1 Pet. 2:17, *NIV*), to "honor those in authority" (see Rom. 13:1-6) and to "honor the brotherhood" (see 1 Pet. 2:17). The Decalogue (the Ten Commandments) itself contains a precept to "honor your father and your mother" (Exod. 20:12).

The honor enjoined is not the superficial sort easily attained by the presentation of a plaque or the awarding of a testimonial dinner. It is the routine daily respect accorded the dignity of other people that is in view. It requires sensitivity to the self-esteem of other people.

Honoring and respecting others admits to a realization that the most fragile mechanism on this planet is the human ego and to a corresponding awareness that the most potent weapon against the ego is the human tongue. Though insults may be humorous when wielded by a master of balance like Don Rickles at a Hollywood roast, it is impossible to honor people with the insult of malice.

OUR SEARCH FOR RECOGNITION

In *How to Win Friends and Influence People*, Dale Carnegie asserts that the easiest way to penetrate the inner sanctum of an important executive's office or to gain an appointment with him is by indicating that the purpose of your call is to gather information for an article of praise about him or to present him with an invitation to be the honored guest at a testimonial dinner. Carnegie understood that people like to be recognized for their achievements.

I recall being seated at an annual convocation at a college where I had just completed my first year on the faculty. Part of the academic ceremony was given over to the announcements of the elevations in rank of the professors. The strata ranged from *instructor* to *full professor*, and I was serving my apprenticeship on the bottom of the totem pole as an instructor.

I listened eagerly for my name as the promotions were announced and was crestfallen when I realized it was absent from the list. I was particularly troubled because when the president of the institution hired me he told me if I performed well I would be elevated to the rank of assistant professor after the first year.

On numerous occasions throughout the academic year the president had taken me aside to give me compliments for my work. So when I was passed over for promotion I was hurt and confused and went to the president for an explanation. He was embarrassed by the omission and confessed that he did remember his commitment.

But it was a sticky problem, as he had later discovered there was a policy that a faculty member had to be on the staff for a minimum of two years before being eligible for promotion. The president was in an awkward position when the dean informed him of the policy. The dean felt the pain of the president's plight, but was caught in the policy squeeze.

To rectify matters, the dean invited me into his office for a private conference. Stumbling for a graceful exit from the dilemma he said to me, "We have been very impressed with your performance here and in order to enhance your prestige with the student body, we have decided to promote you to the rank of assistant professor."

He went on to explain the matter of the policy and the error of the president and concluded his remarks by saying, "Since this goes against faculty policy, we will have to keep this a secret between us as there can be no formal announcement about it."

The compromise was clear; I was to be promoted but in secrecy. Having forgotten his original gambit, the dean turned crimson when I begged the obvious question, "If the reason for the promotion is to give me prestige, with whom will I have it if nobody knows about it?"

Then we both held our sides as we roared in laughter at the humor of the whole thing.

Secret recognition does not do the job. It is recognition before one's peers that enhances self-esteem. The awarding of trophies and medals can be far more valuable to the recipients than their monetary cost. Tokens become treasures when they carry the symbolic clout of recognition.

The gold watch for loyal service, the plaque commemorating participation in a civic project, the diamond ring signaling visible commitment to the engaged woman—all are symbols which capture emotion in tangible form. They guarantee a niche in a special group of people; they carve our names into a timeless tree; they paint a portrait in the faceless crowd; they testify, "I am somebody."

Pat Conroy, in his epic novel *The Lords of Discipline*, describes the moment when the military college senior is awarded his coveted ring:

> My hand felt different as I looked at the ring for the first time. I studied its adroit, inexorable images and translated the silent eloquence of its mythology and language so simply and unceasingly uttered in gold. Until this moment an essential part of me, some vital and unnamable center, had never felt that I was really part of the school. But now the cold gleam of the ring had enclosed me, bound me, and linked me to the Line, for as long as I lived. My hand had sprung suddenly alive as though I had taken its existence for granted. The ring on my finger made an articulate statement; it conveyed a piece of extraordinarily important information to me. It said—no, it shouted out—that Will McLean had added his weight and his story and his own bruised witness to the history of the ring, to the meaning of the ring, and its symbolism. I had encoded my own

messages, scripts, and testimonies into the blazonry of the ring. I studied my new identity, my validation, and I felt changed, completely transfigured in the surprising grandeur of its gold. I was part of it. I had made it.[3]

It might be helpful to go back and read the excerpt again as Conroy captures the power of the symbol of human recognition. It is the green jacket of the Masters golf champion, the Olympic gold medal, the Oscar, the Phi Beta Kappa key, the Superbowl ring and the Nobel Prize all wrapped into one. These things are inestimable in value.

Some people are so gifted and talented that they receive a surplus of honor. Most people spend their days under a cloak of anonymity, hungry for crumbs of honor which may fall their way. Theirs is a surplus of criticism which crushes their spirits an inch at a time.

One psychologist worked out a calculus of criticism and praise by which he argued that it takes nine compliments to undo the pain of one criticism. Our minds tend to fix on the negative when it is directed at us. The minister who hears 50 compliments for his sermon can have his afternoon meal soured by one burning criticism.

Every human being has something about him that is praiseworthy. The genuine compliment is one that crystalizes the strength of a person in words as trophies inscribe it in silver. To be recognized as one who is esteemed, who has worth, is to feel the heady exultation of discovery. We cry with Archimedes, "Eureka! I have found it!"

FOR FURTHER REFLECTION

1. How does your work affect your self-dignity?
2. Where are your aspirations for significance invested?
3. What are the status symbols of your community and work?

4. What kind of bullies do you encounter in your community and workplace?
5. What are the most meaningful compliments you've ever received? Who gave them?
6. What are the most powerful insults or criticisms you've ever received? Who gave them?
7. How do you handle constructive criticism?
8. How do you rate the recognition level you receive for your work?
9. What are your most important tokens or symbols of esteem? Why?
10. What are your greatest achievements? Your worst failures?

CHAPTER TWO

OUR SEARCH FOR LOVE

I remember the first time I said to a girl, "I love you." It happened on a Saturday afternoon in 1951. I was 12 years old. These were the "happy days" when every Saturday afternoon was spent at the local theater enjoying the double-feature matinee for the admission price of 35 cents. We sat in the darkness of the back row, holding hands with our girlfriends, as we beheld the antics of Humphrey Bogart, Alan Ladd, Tyrone Power, Errol Flynn and Francis the Talking Mule.

This day marked a major advance toward manhood as I progressed beyond the puppy love of hand-holding. Surreptitiously, I moved my right arm to the backrest of my girl's seat. I was thrilled to my socks with the move, but it forced me into a difficult position in which to eat my popcorn. I froze in this position staring rigidly forward toward the screen, not daring to glance over to see if my girlfriend had noticed my amorous move.

As the film progressed, probably one of those Jennifer Jones-Joseph Cotton love stories, I began to plan my strategy for declaring my affection with the magic words. "As soon as I finish my popcorn I'll tell her," I vowed to myself.

But when the last kernel was gone (finished by a dexterous left-handed action while holding the bag squeezed between my side and the edge of my seat), my courage failed me. Instead, I spoke such chivalrous words as, "How do you like the movie?"

By now my right arm was closer to the back of her neck as my left hand went to work on the Jujyfruits. Three more self-imposed deadlines came and went as the candy lay heavy in my stomach. Somewhere in the middle of the second feature the words popped out. "I love you."

Now it was her turn to play with her pom-poms as she said not a word. She didn't even squeeze my hand but fixed her eyes on the screen like a zombie.

Am I the only person to ever have those words choke in his mouth? I doubt it. They can be excruciatingly difficult to say and even more difficult to understand.

I think of another movie with Burt Lancaster flashing his whited teeth, playing the role of Elmer Gantry, the flamboyant road-show evangelist. Gantry's game was to open his revival meetings with the question, "What is love?" He was quick to provide a slick answer in the style of the demagogue: "Love is the morning and the evening star; the inspiration of the poets; the substance of the philosophers."

As a tool to manipulate an audience, love becomes just another cheap four-letter word. It can be a buzz word, dying the death of a thousand qualifications. Overused and abused, love has become almost empty of meaning. Yet the sound of the word is still able to cast a spell on the human heart.

When Jesus of Nazareth spoke about love He was not referring to romance or hand-holding in a movie theater. He used it in patterns which are strangely different from the ordinary language of our culture.

PASSIVE AND ACTIVE LOVE

What is the difference in active and passive love?

When Our Love Is Passive

In our society *love* is a feeling word with its power usually described in passive terms. That is, love is something that happens to us over which we have no control. It is like being bitten by a mosquito or attacked by a flu virus. We are victims of its irresistible force and cannot choose to make it come or go willy-nilly.

The college student returns to the fraternity house after dating an exciting coed. Intoxicated by his emotions, he greets his friends with a transparent stare. He blurts out, "It happened! Zing went the strings of my heart."

Pierced in the breast by an arrow from the quiver of Cupid, he speaks of "falling" in love. The songwriter captured the idea when he wrote, "I didn't slip, I wasn't pushed, I *fell* in love."

The lyrics of love put the accent on the passive. In these terms love is spontaneous; no voluntary decision is made, no switch is turned, no button is pressed. It just happens.

The character of passive love is illustrated in an anecdote told by Dr. Jay Adams. Adams tells the story of a man deeply burdened by a failing marriage who visited his minister for pastoral counsel. He explained his predicament by telling the clergyman that love had exited from his marriage and he was considering divorce.

He looked to the pastor for any small portent of hope that the marriage might still be salvaged. The pastor gave his advice in simple terms. "Sir, the Bible says that husbands must love their wives. Therefore, it is your Christian duty to go home and start loving your wife."

The man was incredulous. "How can I do that? That is precisely the problem. That's why I came to you in the first place.

The fact is, I don't love my wife any more. That's why I want out. Can't you give me any better advice?"

The pastor was undeterred by the man's rejection of his counsel, but took a different tact. He suggested an alternate plan: "Why don't you try a trial separation? Try moving next door for a few weeks and see if that helps."

The man was growing impatient and shot back, "What good will that do? How can living next door help?"

In biblical categories, love functions more as a verb than as a noun. It is more concerned with doing than with feelings; it is defined by action.

The pastor replied, "Doesn't God command us to love our neighbors? Maybe if you lived as a next-door neighbor for a while, you would learn to love her again."

The man groaned, "Sir, you don't understand what I'm saying. It's not that a romantic fire has gone out and I need a little space to get it ignited again. The fact is I can't stand the woman. I can't bear the thought of even living in the same neighborhood with her."

"Ahh," sighed the minister. "Now I understand. What you're saying is that your estrangement is so deep you are feeling hostile toward her."

"Bingo! Reverend, now you're catching on."

The minister remained undaunted as he pursued his original course. "May I interpret your remarks to mean that you feel a deep-rooted enmity toward your wife?"

The man allowed the inference.

"Then," said the minister, "let me remind you that God commands us to love our enemies!"

Exasperated, the man walked away sorrowfully, shaking his head. How can one argue with a minister like that?

The point of the anecdote is simple. How absurd it would be to try to obey the divine mandate to love if love were conceived in strictly passive terms. It would make of God a diabolical tyrant who commands the impossible and reduces His precepts to mockery.

When Our Love Is Active

In biblical categories, love functions more as a verb than as a noun. It is concerned more with doing than with feelings; it is defined by action. Love may or may not include warm feelings of affection. When affection is present, that is a bonus, but love can perform without those feelings.

The mandate "Husbands, love your wives" (Eph. 5:25) may be interpreted, "Husbands, *be loving* to your wives." The same may be said of loving one's neighbor (see Mark 12:31) or one's enemies (see Matt. 5:44).

The love which God requires a husband to show to his wife takes its cue from the supreme example of Christ's love for His Church (see Eph. 5:25). That love was made concrete in the sacrifice of giving. Hence, husbands are called to "give themselves" to their wives. The Elizabethan English translation of love was by the word *charity*. Here the link between loving and sacrificial giving is made clear.

God's love is love in action, a love which works in concrete deeds. His love is not static, mirroring the god of Aristotle who is described as "divine thought thinking of itself."[1] A purely passive love is as deadly as an electrical bug killer which entices the night moth by its glowing light only to fry its wings at the slightest touch.

The love of God is not aloof, withdrawn to the isolation of a distant Olympus—He descends from the clouds, wooing and pursuing His people, showing up in the valley of the shadow of death, visiting the house of grief, adding a note of frolic in times of celebration. Love which is passive only is a dead love, indeed no love at all but a mere indulgence in warm feelings. Love is not born until the passive becomes active, the feeling moves to action as the heart moves the feet toward the house of the beloved.

LOYAL LOVE

The love of God by which all human love is measured is closely related to the Hebrew concept of loyalty. To Old Testament Jews, loyalty had a pregnant meaning. It was at the core of their understanding of religion.

It would be a mistake to reduce all religion to a single essence such as loyalty, but it is hard to exaggerate its importance. When we reduce the sum of religious faith to one element we flirt with the error of oversimplification. It is like the exchange which took place between the learned theologian and the distinguished professor of astronomy.

The astronomer was disdainful of religion, poking fun at the theologian for making simple matters so complicated. He said, "You theologians merely confuse people with your complex theories of supralapsarianism, eschatology, ubiquity and forensic justification. To me religion is simple; it's the Golden Rule, 'Do unto others as you would have others do unto you.'"

"I think I understand what you mean," replied the theologian. "I have a similar frustration with astronomers. You fellows confuse me with your theories of expanding universes, galactical perturbations and exploding novae. For me astronomy is very simple, it's 'Twinkle, twinkle little star....'"

The Heart of Loyal Love
There are times in the Bible when important summaries are made. Jesus summarized the whole Law by using the Great

Commandment. James summarized true religion by pointing to the care of widows and orphans.

The summary which puts a heavy accent on loyalty is found in the writings of the prophet Micah. Micah gives God's answer to the basic question, "What does the Lord require of you?" by writing the summary response: "To do justice, and to love kindness, and to walk humbly with your God" (6:8, *RSV*).

The summary lays bare the heart of biblical love. We like to have things boiled down as we seek to learn things quickly in three easy lessons. Micah does the job for us by spelling it out in simple terms.

What does God want from us?

- *The first requirement is "to do justice."*

    God wants from us a passion for justice and righteousness; not merely our theoretical interest in justice, but that we *do* justice.

    Jesus echoed this priority when He summarized the Beatitudes by saying, "Seek ye first the kingdom of God, and his righteousness; and all these things shall be added unto you" (Matt. 6:33, *KJV*).
- *The second requirement is "to love kindness."*

    Here we encounter the loyalty factor. In other translations, "to love kindness" is rendered by the phrases "to love mercy" or "to act with steadfast love" or "to love loyally." The same Hebrew word is used for *mercy, steadfast love* and *loyal love*, as these elements blend together in a single potent word.

    Loyalty is built on steadfast love, a love which does not crumble with the first insult or failure. Loyal love is a love we can count on.
- *The third requirement is "to walk humbly with your God."*

The words are simple but they sound out the depths of theological waters. To walk humbly with God assumes one understands who God is.

It implies a recognition of His sovereign authority. It bows before His omniscience, submitting in proper humility to His divine right to impose obligations upon us and set commandments before us. It presupposes that we understand that we are creatures and He is the Creator. It implies devotion, communion, fellowship—all the things upon which a personal relationship with God is established.

Loyal love embraces the "quality of mercy which is not strained."[2] It is the stuff of which enduring relationships are made.

The Importance of Loyal Love

How important is loyalty to a marriage? To a family? To a soldier? To a business relationship? To ask these simple questions is to answer them.

By the fates of computerized seat selection, I was once thrust into the company of Edward De Bartolo for a transcontinental flight to San Francisco. De Bartolo is the millionaire owner of the twice Super Bowl Champion San Francisco 49ers. Professional football, however, is just one of many De Bartolo enterprises.

During our inflight conversation, I asked him, "What do you regard as the single most important quality you look for in an employee?"

He responded without a moment's hesitation, "Loyalty."

De Bartolo's answer surprised me as I had heard the frequent criticism of bosses who surround themselves with loyal yes-men. But De Bartolo insisted that a loyal friend or employee is anything but a yes-man. There are times when loyalty requires saying no.

It is when we confuse love with indulgence that we think of loyalty as spineless acquiescence to the whim of the leader. I was guilty of that misassociation when I registered shock at De Bartolo's answer.

We hunger for friends who are loyal, but sometimes we are reduced to begging for crumbs to avoid starvation. A leader of a large national Christian organization once remarked to me candidly, "I hope that when I die there will be at least five of my friends who will be able to sit through my funeral service without looking at their watches." The comment was made wistfully, not cynically.

It is difficult to know in advance who will remain loyal in times of crisis. When the crisis comes it usually brings surprises in its wake. People we count on desert us, while others we thought would run away rush to our side.

I spoke to a woman who was crushed by the backfire of expected loyalty. Her son was arrested on a drug charge in the local high school. In her grief about the matter she thought of a good friend whom she assumed would be worried about how the family was handling the crisis. She went to her friend to assure her that she was holding up under the strain.

Her friend said, "You shouldn't be so peaceful. It is your fault this happened." She then unleashed a vicious attack on the woman for being a bad mother whose poor parenting had caused her son's misconduct, bringing a scandal to the whole community.

The Forebearance of Loyal Love

The biblical concept of loyal love is augmented by the statement, "There is a love which covers a multitude of sins" (see 1 Pet. 4:8). On the surface this verse seems to suggest a kind of celestial Watergate, a sanctified covert operation of stonewalling.

But that is not what loyal love is about. Biblically, such love assumes a context of forgiven people who struggle daily to

improve their obedience to God, though frustrated by frequent failures. It speaks of a love which is tolerant and patient, the kind
which is willing to absorb the minor sin. It is aimed at the avoid-
ance of pettiness or of picking at minute faults and weaknesses.

This covering is not a form of indulgence of the serious sin
or the criminal act. Biblical love is what Bill Milliken once wrote
about in his book *Tough Love*. Love demands excellence, and it
affirms people by expecting responsible behavior from them.

ABIDING LOVE

Perhaps the most famous and popular chapter of the entire
New Testament is the "Love Chapter" of 1 Corinthians 13. It
enhances our understanding of biblical love more powerfully
than does any other single piece of literature:

> If I speak in the tongues of men and of angels, but
> have not love, I am only a resounding gong or a clang-
> ing cymbal. If I have the gift of prophecy and can fath-
> om all mysteries and all knowledge, and if I have a
> faith that can move mountains, but have not love, I am
> nothing. If I give all I possess to the poor and surren-
> der my body to the flames, but have not love, I gain
> nothing.
>
> Love is patient, love is kind. It does not envy, it
> does not boast, it is not proud. It is not rude, it is not
> self-seeking, it is not easily angered, it keeps no record
> of wrongs. Love does not delight in evil but rejoices with
> the truth. It always protects, always trusts, always hopes,
> always perseveres.
>
> Love never fails. But where there are prophecies,
> they will cease; where there are tongues, they will be
> stilled; where there is knowledge, it will pass away.

For we know in part and we prophesy in part, but when perfection comes, the imperfect disappears.

When I was a child, I talked like a child, I thought like a child, I reasoned like a child. When I became a man, I put childish ways behind me. Now we see but a poor reflection; then we shall see face to face. Now I know in part; then I shall know fully, even as I am fully known.

And now these three remain: faith, hope and love. But the greatest of these is love (*NIV*).

The lyric sound and rhythmic flow of this passage suggests the ring of poetry. We have heard it recited in dramatic readings by people like Charles Laughton, Rex Harrison and Orson Wells. However, Paul is not waxing eloquent as a poet.

Abiding Love Is Genuine Love

This passage is an integral part of a teaching portion of the Epistle. The purpose is to teach us what genuine love is, not to titillate our aesthetic senses. It is the loftiness of the subject and the beauty of its content which make it easily mistaken for poetry.

Love is compared and contrasted with other spiritual gifts and activities. The teaching is clear: tongues without love is just noise—indeed, an irritating cacophony. Prophetic insight or the acquisition of knowledge and academic brilliance, combined with a mountain-moving faith, add up to zero if love is absent. Philanthropy and martyrdom show a net loss on the balance sheet without the presence of love.

In a word, Christian life without love is an exercise in futility.

Abiding Love Is Durable Love

Love is linked to kindness, patience, protection, trust, hope and perseverance. These touch the time factor of love. The stress is on its durable character.

This is not love at first sight which quickly vanishes at the first sign of trouble. Patient love is not possible without the test of time. Genuine love is a long-term reality.

When I really fell in love for the first time I had reached the mature age of 13. Nat King Cole was going to the top of the

---

Lasting love...is built on the rock base of trust. Trust is a shaky thing, fragile at best. It can take years to develop strength, and moments to be shattered.

---

charts with his hit song "Too Young." The lyrics described my frustration with the older generation to a tee. For they spoke of teenage love which is rudely dismissed by all knowing adults as an empty word and of the passion of the young to prove their elders wrong: to prove that the love of the teenager exceeds that of the puppy.

I was frustrated with my teachers telling me I was too young to know what love was all about. I revered the single exception among adults who at least pretended she believed me. Even my classmates ridiculed my passion.

Still, my zeal was so intense, my conviction so deep that this was the real thing I made a wager with a friend about it. I bet him $10 (that's big-time gambling for a 13-year-old) that I would marry the girl. Eight years later I enclosed with my wedding invitation to that friend, who was foolish enough to be so easily parted from his money, my bill for the $10 he owed me.

All I had to bank on was my emotion, one friendly teacher and the kindly understanding of Nat King Cole. My wife has sometimes wondered if the thing that sustained our lengthy courtship was my fierce desire to win the bet. But now I know, with apologies to the songwriter, that the love I felt at 13 was trivial compared with the kind that has emerged over time.

Abiding Love Is Trusting Love

Lasting love, the kind that is tempered by the crucible of pain and adversity, is built on the rock base of trust. Trust is a shaky thing, fragile at best. It can take years to develop strength, and moments to be shattered.

So abiding love must be able to endure disappointments and being let down at points by people we count on. It does not refer to blind credulity born of naivete. We know people are sinful, and that knowledge makes it foolish to look at the world and its people through rose-tinted spectacles.

The Judgment of Charity. The judgment of charity is the evaluation of other people which is tempered by love. It freely gives the benefit of the doubt while fleeing the temptation toward heartless and cruel denunciation. It is a love free of envy and malice.

The Puritan teacher Jonathan Edwards said:

> If love is the sum of Christianity, surely those things which overthrow love are exceedingly unbecoming to Christians. An envious Christian, a malicious Christian, a cold and hard-hearted Christian, is the greatest absurdity and contradiction. It is as if one should speak of dark brightness, or a false truth.[3]

For trusting love to survive the conflicts and clashes which assault every human relationship, we need to acquire a benefit of the doubt posture, a skill of rendering the judgment of charity. Conceding this truth means then that the single essential ingredient to abiding love is the practice of the judgment of charity.

But how does this type of charity work out in practical terms? How we respond to mistreatment from others offers some clues.

Only yesterday I hastened from my lunch table at a restaurant, rushing to the parking lot because I was late for an appointment. When I got to my car I was upset to see that a delivery truck was blocking my exit. I sat behind the wheel, fuming at the thoughtless act of the truck driver. At the height of my growing annoyance I was beginning to take the incident personally as if the driver had stayed up all night plotting to torment me by making me late.

As I cooled off, I noticed that the parking lot was full, it was pouring down rain and there was no other place nearby for the driver to stop to make his delivery. I am sure the driver had hoped that he would be able to return to his truck before the unfortunate owner of the car he was blocking came out of the restaurant. He was as harried as I was. But, within the space of five minutes, my mind had run the gamut from accusing him of the worst possible motives to excusing him with the best of motives.

When we assume the worst motives for pain inflicted upon us, we are resorting to *worst-case analysis*. We overreact, thinking people mean to hurt us as badly as they do. But because they often do not, a common ingredient of the apology is found in the words, "I didn't mean to...."

Sometimes it is hard to accept these words, as we would rather think the offense came with malice aforethought. It rarely does. In the normal give-and-take of human relations much pain is inflicted with no intention of doing so. The thoughtless word and the irresponsible act may be inflicted without malice, though they are no less painful for the lack of intent.

On the opposite end of the spectrum is *best-case analysis*. Here we attribute the best possible motives for an injurious action. Unfortunately, we usually reserve this best-case thinking for the defense of our own misdeeds.

We witnessed a president assuming this posture during the national trauma of Watergate, the political black eye of the century. When the president of the United States was forced to resign because of it, Jimmy Hoffa, former Teamsters union president, remarked, "It's a damn shame to lose the presidency over a third-rate burglary."

But it was not the burglary that cost Richard Nixon his place in the White House. It was the cover-up which followed. The American people could not tolerate being lied to by their president.

When the president appeared on television to confess his misdeed, he said, "I made a mistake." Those four words, more than any other, destroyed the president's chances of being restored to public favor.

There is a huge difference between telling a lie and making a mistake. The difference is moral. When one tells a lie and calls it a mistake he is resorting to best-case analysis.

We can forgive our president for making mistakes, perhaps even for lying to us, but not if he compounds the felony by lying about the lie. One prominent senator said at the time, "If Mr. Nixon had just come on the air and said forthrightly, 'I lied. I'm sorry. Please forgive me' he would have been embraced by a compassionate nation and allowed to stay in office."

Nixon's biggest mistake was in soft-pedaling his confession. And he was deemed an arch villain for doing in a crisis what we all tend to do every day. This is our natural tendency—to view the sins of others with indignation while excusing our own sins by presenting them in the best of all possible lights.

Sometimes we explain our errors in such positive terms that they sound like virtues. It is the familiar pattern by which we are more keenly alert to the speck in our brother's eye than to the log in our own. Usually the truth in painful human conflict lies somewhere between worse-case and best-case.

Love tends to err in the direction of best-case when evaluating other people's motives. It avoids the slander resulting from worst-case analysis which blackens the evil in the eye of the beholder.

Marriage counselors are acutely aware of the hostility fueled by worst-case analysis. Lovers' quarrels escalate to bitter fights when each party accuses the other of the worst motives. It is tragic to think of the divorces which could be avoided and the destruction of other relationships which would be eliminated if the judgment of charity were practiced in marriage, in friendship or at the bargaining table.

Closely related to the problem of mistrust is the *spirit of retaliation* which seeks revenge for wrongs suffered. A common expression used in our culture is, "Don't get mad, get even." This is the creed of retaliation by which we lash out as a response to pain.

The Desire for Vindication. There is a thin line, sometimes a razor's edge, between the desire for vindication and the desire for revenge, yet it is the difference between virtue and vice. God utters no prohibition against the desire for vindication; rather, He encourages His people to pray for it.

Vengeance is quite another matter. God presents sharp rebuke against the vengeful.

What is the difference between revenge and vindication?

Vindication occurs when a person is cleared of blame. If a person is slanderously accused of an evil for which he is not guilty and then is shown to be innocent, he is vindicated. The slanderer, however, is shown to be guilty. If the injured party then takes it upon himself to punish the slanderer, he moves from vindication to revenge.

Does this mean vengeance is evil and crime should go unpunished? By no means. Vengeance itself must not be seen as an intrinsic evil lest we cast a shadow on the integrity of God. Far from repudiating vengeance as an evil, God appropriates it to Himself saying, "Vengeance is mine. I will repay."

What is most obvious in this saying is often overlooked. It is not a blanket condemnation of all vengeance, but carries the clear and certain divine pledge that vengeance will be exacted. The promise is unequivocal. "I will repay."

What is vital about God's Word is that He reserves the role of avenger to Himself and to those to whom He delegates that responsibility. God limits vengeance by establishing the boundaries of its implementation. It belongs to Him and not to the individual to avenge the crimes committed.

God delegates and assigns the responsibility of vengeance in the exacting of justice to human courts of law. They too are held accountable to God for how they carry out their responsibility. The principle remains intact: the individual is not to be the agent of his own revenge.

The vendetta is excluded from our options.

With this restriction, the perfect wisdom of God is manifest. Who among us has either the wisdom or the restraint necessary to exact a perfectly proportionate measure of justice for the wrongs we suffer? We move too easily across the line to injustice by imposing punishments more severe than the crime.

The sentiment "Don't get mad, get even" reveals not so much a desire for justice as a hunger for retaliation. It tends toward overkill, and the Deity knows it.

Few have the grace to resist the drive for vengeance. A noteworthy example of such extraordinary grace is seen in a case involving the New England scholar Jonathan Edwards. Edwards, along with John Wesley and Charles Whitfield, was a driving force behind the "Great Awakening" of eighteenth-century America. His preaching captivated his congregation, rendering them stunned, even though his sermons were delivered in a monotone.

Not all those present in his Northhampton parish were enamored of his spiritual leadership. One gentleman developed a bitter dislike for Edwards and undertook a plan to overthrow his ministry. In a clear case of malice aforethought, the man stealthily planted rumors of a slanderous nature designed to undermine Edwards's reputation and impugn his personal character. This was welcome grist in the gossip-mongers' mill, and in short time vicious tales were circulated through the town.

With a public aroused by the defaming gossip, some of the leaders of the church came to Edwards urging him to answer the

---

Sometimes we emulate the Pharisees more than we imitate Christ.

---

calumnious charges publicly. Edwards steadfastly refused to speak a word in his own defense.

When the scandal reached fiery proportions, one of Edwards's friends approached him and said, "Jonathan, what's the matter with you? Don't you want to be vindicated of these charges?"

Edwards replied, "I certainly do. I want it very badly."

"Then why won't you speak in your own defense?" the man entreated.

Edwards spoke again, "Does not God promise to vindicate His people? I prefer His vindication to my own. Perhaps if I defend myself, God will allow that to be the extent of my defense; but if I remain silent, then God will move heaven and earth to secure my vindication. I am confident that His vindication of me will far exceed any attempts of my own."

God did move heaven and earth to vindicate His servant. Time passed before it happened, but the guilty man became so troubled by the enormity of his abusive act, and doubly shamed by Edwards's silence, that he came forth and publicly made a full confession of his lies. Edwards experienced in this world the vindicating power of God's steadfast love.

PERFECT LOVE

First Corinthians 13 tells us that love does not envy, boast or exhibit pride. It is not rude, self-seeking or easily angered. It keeps no record of wrongs and does not delight in evil (see vv. 4,5).

Perfect Love Renounces Self

These characteristics are the *abstentions of perfect love.* And they contain a common thread of vice woven by self-centeredness. So these are not the external taboos which masquerade in moralist circles as the touchstone of true religion. For love is not defined by simplistic abstinence from dancing, movies, card-playing and the like.

Rudeness required the Cross, not lipstick; covetousness demanded atonement, not pinochle; pride called forth propitiation, not the cinema. Sometimes we emulate the Pharisees more than we imitate Christ who rebuked His complacent contemporaries for omitting "the weightier matters of the law, justice and mercy and faith" (Matt. 23:23, *RSV*).

Some describe true love as "unconditional love." The concept can be a golden coin or a gilded rock in the fraud's bag of tricks. Such love can ring with the clink of sound metal or echo the thud of the counterfeit mixed with dross. For unconditional love is at once true and grossly false depending upon how it is understood.

The preacher who smiles benignly from his pulpit assuring us that "God accepts you just the way you are" tells a monstrous lie. He sugarcoats the gospel of love with saccharine grace. God does not accept the arrogant; He turns His back to the impenitent. He maintains love toward His fallen creatures, inviting them back to restored fellowship, but strings are securely attached for we must come on bended knee.

Perfect Love Overcomes Prejudice

We all participate in the universal infection of prejudice. The conditions we attach to our love are not always as holy as God's. Ours flow from bigotry and fears of those different from us or those too much like us.

I have an allergy to cowards. I find them difficult to like. I applauded George C. Scott as he acted out the infamous moment in the career of General Patton when Patton slapped the cowardly soldier.

My antipathy toward cowards has twin roots:

The *first root* grows from my own fears so easily awakened within me. Cowardice is contagious and I fear infection from those who host a lethal dose.

I admire courage and require the bolstering which comes from contact with courageous people. They are not fearless, else they could have no courage. Fear is the prime requisite of courage, for without fear courage would be superfluous.

Anyone can act when he is not afraid. It is when fear strikes that the battle between cowardice and courage begins. When the bugle sounds, the coward collapses and the courageous man does precisely the thing he is afraid to do.

The *second root* is resentment aimed at those who have fled the battle scene and have played collaborator to the enemy. It was the context that troubled Patton so, as he found the coward not trembling in solitude but in the midst of a field hospital which housed the battered bodies of the valiant ones.

Perfect love overcomes these prejudices, helping us to snip the strings we attach to love. Love means resisting the imposing of conditions on other people before we are willing to respect them.

We do not have to admire people or even like them to treat them with respect. Cowards have dignity and should not be written off for one moment of paralysis under fire. Even the Wizard of Oz understood that.

BLIND LOVE

In the drama of romance we are often confounded by the ability of love to see beyond ugliness to beauty. A frequent remark we hear on the grapevine of community gossip is "I wonder what she sees in him." Sight alone cannot explain why people fall in love.

The perception of the soul goes beyond the heart of darkness to explore the majesty of hidden personality. What is it that enabled the grotesquely deformed "Elephant Man"[4] to look at his wretched face in the mirror and say, "I am a man"?

Looking Beyond Ugliness to Beauty

The love that looks beyond ugliness was taught me most poignantly not by a person, but by a dog. His name was Hosannah, dubbed by the breeder for his distinction of being born on Palm Sunday. He was a German Shepherd puppy, boasting of the finest blood lines—a sable son of champions, the offspring of the Canadian Grand Victor.

Our family welcomed him as he was presented to us as a gift upon our arrival in the Ligonier Valley in 1971. He was four months old at the time, already displaying the proud bearing of his line and the unusually gentle disposition of his father.

I was stricken with horror only one week later when I found the dog in our driveway, writhing in agony, his head swollen to twice its normal size. I rushed him to the veterinarian, assuming that the only possible cause for the swelling was an encounter with a hornet's nest and the subsequent assault of multiple stings. I was wrong.

The doctor's careful probing revealed three distinct marks on the dog's head and face. They were fang marks, left from the strikes of a deadly copperhead snake. "Hosie" hovered near death for two weeks with antidotes battling the venom in his body.

I was joyous when the vet called to announce that the dog would live and that I could come to the animal hospital to take him home for further recuperation. But I was not prepared for the visual shock that greeted me when I went to pick him up. He had no face—it was gone.

The effect of the poison was to cause necrosis, the rotting of the skin tissue which covered his face. The sinews of muscle were bare to the naked eye, the sinus cavities were exposed to the air. The sight was made more miserable when coupled with the offense to the nostrils of the stench of rotting tissue.

My first thought was, "Why didn't he let him die?"

The doctor explained that the dog's face would eventually heal. He gave me plastic gloves and a large jar of ointment to apply to his face three times a day to hasten the healing process. The dog was silent and immobile, as if shrinking in shame. He seemed to sense the loss of his canine beauty.

At home we prepared a recovery room for him in our garage where the putrid odor of his wounds would not penetrate the house. I cringed as I entered the garage and pulled the plastic gloves over my fingers. Nausea filled my weak stomach when I scooped a handful of ointment from the jar and approached the animal.

A piece of flesh was dangling from his forehead, like a flap covering his eye, giving the appearance that the dog's eye had fallen from its socket. Without rational thought, I instinctively studied the floor for the missing eyeball. My brain registered revulsion as I realized my error.

I held my breath while I touched his face, gently applying the salve, eager to complete the task. But something happened when the dog looked at me with saddened eyes, holding his face steady as I applied the treatment. It was as if he understood how difficult it was for me to do it and as if he were trying to tell me "thank you" for caring.

Somehow communication took place between man and

beast, and I was no longer aware of either the offensive sight or smell. I made the next application of the ointment with my bare hands, tenderly administering it without a trace of repugnance.

Within two months the dog's face healed. The open cavities were sealed over with a hard leathery layer of black scar tissue. The scar tissue twisted his face into what some perceived as a frozen snarl, but which we preferred to regard as a perpetual smile.

Hosie and I became inseparable companions as he walked where I walked and slept by my side when I stood at the podium to deliver my lectures. Nature gave him genes to care for sheep but he thought he was a bird dog. He leapt with joy when I went to the gun cabinet to select my equipment for the exhilarating hunt for grouse in the upland thickets of the mountains behind our house. He loved the woods, being both excited and befuddled by the exploding thunder of the flushing birds.

My shotgun and I were but minor annoyances to the grouse who always eluded me. I swear some stopped bothering to fly, choosing instead the donning of earmuffs when they saw me coming. But it was great fun to tiptoe silently through the woods with Hosie at my side.

Our love relationship between man and dog lasted two years. Finally the residual effects of the toxins in his body became manifest. Hosie began to suffer convulsions, rendered helpless by violent seizures occurring five and six times a day. No medicine was found to control the debilitating malady and the vet made the grim suggestion, couched in euphemism, that Hosie be "put to sleep."

My options were few. I could take the dog for an innocent walk in the woods, turning my gun on him when he wasn't looking; but I knew such a deed was beyond me. I could put him in the car and drive to the animal hospital, paying $35 for the painless injection that would end his life. I chose neither.

Instead I said to my wife, "Ask one of the students to drive

Hosie to the vet this week. Don't tell me what day. Don't tell me until it's over."

I could not bear riding in the car with Hosie, knowing inside I was taking him to his death. He was ugly, but I no longer noticed. I loved him.

Exploring the Majesty of Hidden Personality

I had a college student who was a victim of cerebral palsy. He was able to walk, but with great difficulty as his legs and arms would fly in all directions, out of control of the motor impulses which make walking a normally simple task. His speech was slurred, slow and agonizing, demanding great concentration on the part of the listener to understand. There was nothing wrong with his mind, however, and his sparkling personality and spontaneous smile were an inspiration to his classmates and to all who encountered him.

One day he came to me vexed by a problem and asked me to pray for him. In the course of the prayer, I said something routine, with words like, "Oh, God, please help this man as he wrestles with his problem." When I opened my eyes the student was quietly weeping.

I asked him what was wrong and he stammered his reply, "You called me a man—no one has ever called me a man before."

MATURE LOVE

Mature, Not Perfect

No one possesses perfect love now, but the apostle says, "Love never fails" (1 Cor. 13:8, *NIV*). That is hard to hear. My love fails, and I have been flunked out of the school of other people's love.

But Paul is speaking here of Love with a capital *L*. The love of God has no terminal point. It does not quit.

God's love has the power of eternal endurance. No creaturely act can bring God's love to ruin; it simply cannot perish. Only in heaven will we be able to offer a completed reflection of the love of God.

Paul stresses the mature character of love. Though perfection is out of reach, maturity is not. It is mature love that goes the second mile, that is willing to absorb the pain of conflict. Mature love is patient with the wayward child and the troublesome employee.

Childlike, Not Childish
There are times God calls us to be childlike; but childlikeness must not be confused with childishness. New Testament love is not made of plastic but is the sort that has passed through the fire. It has undergone the sting of the tragic and has prevailed.

Maturity requires a putting away of childish ways. The pouting, the tantrums, the whining, all have to go.

Mature love is desperately needed in our broken world. Our search for dignity is a cruel joke without the presence of this ingredient. Just as every person wants to be treated with respect, so also every person wants to be loved. We crave it.

No wonder the apostle concludes his exhortation by saying, "So faith, hope, love abide, these three; but the greatest of these is love" (1 Cor. 13:13, *RSV*).

THE HEALING OF BROKEN LOVE

One of the first nursery rhymes we learn as children concerns the sad plight of Humpty Dumpty. He is portrayed as an egglike gnome who suffers a tragic fall from his precarious perch on the wall. The brittle shell of his body shatters on impact with the ground. The delicate pieces are so fragmented, so scattered about, that the combined forces of the kingdom lack the power and skill to restore him to wholeness.

We feel like the mythical Dumpty when a friendship is destroyed and love is broken. The shattering of the relationship seems final, with no power available to mend it.

Reconciliation Means Mediating Estranged Relationships

A word we hear, sprinkled profusely throughout sacred Scripture, frightens us a bit because it has the power of conjuring up hope when we are afraid to hope. It beckons us as a seductive lantern in the fog, luring us, we fear, to further ruin or hidden rocks. It sounds too much like a magic elixir, a potent medicine which promises the cure-all of the road-show quack or the heartless charlatan.

The word is *reconciliation*. And, though we may be hesitant in appropriating it for ourselves, the word is holy and made dignified by its central importance to the ministry of Christ whom some do not believe but none dare call a quack.

Reconciliation means bringing people together in peace; people who were once estranged from each other. Estrangement is the one indispensable ingredient for reconciliation, for without it no reconciliation is needed. Estrangement is the shattering blow which makes reconciliation necessary if peace is to be achieved and love restored.

Christ was not a dabbler in mediation. He majored in it, thrusting the task of mediation and peacemaking to center stage in the work of His Church. His mission gives the cue to our mission.

The mission of Christ was made necessary by human estrangement. We are told that alienation exists on three levels:

> In the first instance, man is alienated from God.
> In the second instance, man is alienated from his fellow man.
> In the third instance, man is alienated from himself.

These three levels are intimately related to each other. For complete reconciliation to take place, it must happen at all three levels.

Man's estrangement from God splinters all other human relationships. This primary fracture splinters all other human relationships as it reflects a distortion to the whole of human life. As Saint Augustine stated in *The Confessions,* "O Lord, thou hast made us for thyself and our hearts are restless until they find their rest in thee."

This restlessness penetrates to the core of the human soul. One of the dominant themes of the existentialist philosopher is the pervasive problem of human anxiety. This *angst* of which the philosophers speak is traced to man's awareness of his finitude or of his dread of death.

The theologian takes it a step further and locates it in the primordial sphere of man's broken fellowship with his Creator. This anxiety is usually experienced as a vague, amorphous kind of restlessness. It differs from the specified fear associated with particular phobias such as fear of the dark, fear of heights or fear of crowded spaces.

This fearful restlessness is a haunting type of dread that makes us afraid of we know not what. It may present itself in a form of hostility toward God or the things of God. We may experience a kind of cosmic paranoia where we feel the angry breath of God on the back of our necks when He is not on the hunt.

Martin Luther described this fear when he said, "The pagan trembles at the rustling of a leaf," and which the Bible speaks of when it says, "The wicked flee when no one pursues" (Prov. 28:1, *RSV*).

When our sacred relationship with God is exploded we experience a consequent fallout in human relationships. The biblical account of the Fall is closely followed by the first example in the history of fratricide. The murder of Abel at the hands of Cain was the earth's first baptism of human blood. That blood cried out to God as human reconciliation was instantly a major crisis.

Since that earliest estrangement, the earth has been drenched with the blood flowing from human hatred and hostility. We live in a culture torn by strife at every level of human relationship. The divorce rate measuring marriages broken by estrange-

---

The ultimate paradigm of reconciliation is seen in the figure of Christ upon the Cross.

---

ment approaches the 50 percent mark. We face bitter hostility between racial groups, political dissidents, teachers and students, employers and employees, and parents and children. Ours is an age bathed in anger with terrorism growing in intensity as a modern response to estrangement; an age screaming for mediation.

The role of the mediator resembles that of a lightning rod. For he is frequently called upon to stand in the middle between angry and opposing forces, absorbing much of the hostility himself. The life of a mediator can be as dangerous as the life of a referee in the National Hockey League. Yet serving as a mediator is the price that must be paid if one is genuinely concerned for reaching reconciliation.

The ultimate paradigm of reconciliation is seen in the figure of Christ upon the Cross. In His moment of agony, Christ exposed Himself not only to the unbridled hostility of angry men, but, more significantly, to the unmitigated wrath of God. He became the target of both sides of the divine/human estrangement and absorbed it in Himself.

Reconciliation Means Understanding the Roots of Anger
If the mediator is to be effective, he must first learn to understand

anger. He must be able to distinguish between different types and levels of hostility if he is called to stand in the middle of it. Estrangement manifests itself outwardly in anger which can easily be elevated to such a fever pitch that it expresses itself in violence.

The roots of anger are almost always found in some kind of pain. That pain can proceed from physical injury or from emotional upsets of frustration and disappointment:

> If someone were to strike us on the face, the most likely immediate response to the stinging blow would be anger.
>
> If we seek diligently to achieve a goal, only to lose it in the end, we experience the pain of frustration.
>
> If we have our hearts set on something which fails to materialize, we learn the pain of disappointment.

Too much frustration or an overdose of disappointment can produce anger that yields an abiding bitterness by which personalities are soured.

We think of the violence that sometimes erupts in the midst of professional football games or hockey games when tempers flare and players begin to trade punches. It seems odd that grown men, who are paid professionals, would behave in such a manner. These athletes are not only well-conditioned physically, but must learn self-control, keeping their emotions in harness in order to execute their plays properly.

They are disciplined daily by handling the physical blows that are an integral part of a game. Why then do they sometimes explode in anger during a game and overreact to a physical hit? The question could be stated, *When* do the tempers flare and the athletes lose their poise?

The majority of fights occur in the fourth quarter of the game when it becomes apparent to one team that they are going to lose. It is the bitterness of defeat and the frustration that is carried in its wake, that break down the discipline. When the awareness of defeat dawns, the pain of every normal blow becomes intensified and anger escalates to the boiling point.

Consider also the emotional behavior of the child who receives the diabolical gift of the playbench with multiformed holes in it. Some of the holes in the bench—seemingly designed by the Marquis de Sade—are round, some oblong, some triangular and some square. All the little tyke has to do is figure out which peg fits in which hole.

Watch the child as he patiently tries to pound the round peg into the square hole. The game starts in a spirit of mirth but quickly becomes earnest as the peg will not cooperate. Finally, the child begins to pound the hammer furiously as his emotions take on the level of rage. He throws the hammer on the ground, starts shaking his fists and stomping his feet as he lets out a shriek of protest.

Intrinsically, nothing is wrong with anger. Anger, in itself, is a neutral emotion. We are not only permitted to get angry, but at least one Bible injunction enjoins it. The apostle Paul writes, "Be angry...." And the verb is in the imperative. He hastens, however, to add the qualifying words, "but [in your anger] do not sin; do not let the sun go down on your anger" (Eph. 4:26, *RSV*).

If anger were conceived of as an intrinsic evil, to attribute it to God would be blasphemy. Yet, the biblical God is capable of holy wrath which Jesus Himself more than once displayed. Anger at times is justified and appropriate.

Anger, however, is a dangerous emotion as it easily becomes an occasion for sin. Anger that rages out of control can become violent and destructive. Anger that abides after the sun has set can turn into bitterness.

There are a lot of angry people in the world. Too many sunsets have hardened the hearts of multitudes. The child psychologist knows that the principal cause of teenage rebellion is unresolved anger. The delinquent child is almost always the angry child.

Understanding the roots of that anger is necessary before there can be any real hope of reconciliation between parent and child. Understanding the child's pain can also serve to increase our own patience toward his unpleasant behavior.

While in seminary, I was employed in an inner-city recreation program for youth. My responsibility was to supervise the basketball program in a local gymnasium. I found one youngster there so difficult to like that he cast serious doubts on the credibility of Father Edward J. Flanagan, the founder of Boys Town, who asserted, "There's no such thing as a bad boy."

This particular boy was an irritant to me and a source of trouble for the other children. He made his presence felt as an incorrigible bully.

One afternoon my attention was wrenched to a far corner of the gym by a horrible scream. As I rushed to investigate, I saw a shy boy cowering in the corner beside a model airplane he was working on. The bully screamed that his eyes were burning and he could not see. The bully had been tormenting the younger boy who, in frustration, resorted to throwing a bottle of acid into the face of his tormentor.

I scooped the bully in my arms and rushed him to the washroom to apply wet compresses to his eyes. Alerting someone to call the hospital, I carried the boy to my car and rushed to the emergency room. When an injured child is brought into the emergency room of a city hospital there is an added pace of urgency. The treatment was swift and effective, as a quick analysis of the acidic substance was made and countermeasures taken to neutralize the effects.

After two anxious hours the boy was returned to my care to be delivered home. His head was swathed in bandages with one eye completely covered. He looked like a refugee from the *Spirit of '76*, but, otherwise, he was pronounced fit to go home.

On the drive home, the boy was reluctant to talk and asked me to drop him off about a block from his residence. I explained that it was necessary for me to deliver him to his parents. He related that he lived alone with his mother because his father had left long ago. A long line of "uncles," he said, periodically came and went, sometimes spending the night.

I began to get the picture. The boy grew increasingly apprehensive as we approached his street. To get to his home, we had to climb three flights of outside stairs to the entrance of a shoddy tenement.

When his mother came to the door she said nothing to me as she took in the sight of her son wrapped in bandages. I expected her to cry in horror or to grab him and smother him with kisses. Instead, she unleashed a verbal barrage of obscenities directed at her son.

He shrank in embarrassment that I should be a witness to this tongue-lashing. The mother curtly dismissed me as she jerked the boy's arm and dragged him inside to continue her verbal abuse.

I found the scene barely possible to comprehend. Suddenly I saw the boy in quite a different light. He was clearly an emotionally battered child whose background did not excuse his belligerent behavior, but certainly made it easier to understand. I gained a new facility for patience with him. The venom he poured out on other children was his outward expression of inward wounds.

Reconciliation Means Looking for the Pain Beneath the Anger

All sorts of hidden wounds are carried about by the people we deal with daily. It is not everyone's role to be a practicing psychologist, but there are basic patterns of human behavior we can all be aware of. The principle rule for the mediator is, *When anger is present, look for the pain.*

Dealing with the pain that lies beneath the surface of anger is far less volatile than dealing directly with the anger. It is normal to respond to anger with anger and escalate hostility to the level of violence.

The wisdom literature of the Old Testament contains the proverb, "A soft answer turneth away wrath" (Prov. 15:1, *KJV*). Its antithetical corollary would be, "A harsh answer compounds

---

Once God reconciles a person to Himself, He does not adopt a posture of belligerence, poised to strike the instant we step out of line.

---

wrath." Angry responses to anger is like iron against iron, with each blow cutting deeper and the chasm of estrangement growing wider.

The marriage counselor is familiar with the typical course of domestic arguments. People begin to speak *at* each other rather than *to* each other, missing the concealed pain. It is one thing for a spouse to say, "You make me mad." It is quite another to say, "You have hurt me."

What makes unresolved anger dangerous is where it is carried and to whom it is applied. If a person is frustrated all day at work, it is natural for him to carry his anger home and make his family the victims of it. Conversely, domestic quarrels have a way of being carried out of the home and into the workplace.

The anger that boils in the work world is not of recent origin. The hostility between labor and management has simmered over many years of heated combat. The Homestead "Battle of the Barges"[5] that rocked the nation happened decades ago and became a pivotal point in the history of the labor movement. Too many brickbats have been thrown, too many contractual disputes have been endured and too many embittered strikes have taken place to expect the fires that presently burn to be cooled overnight.

Reconciliation Means Learning That Adversaries Desire Peace

A mediator must also stand between adversaries. Reconciliation in the work world is made more difficult by the retreat of both sides into their own corners and their adoption of an adversary-style of encounter. Labor perceives management as holding the trump cards of power and imagines their only hope of success is to fight with a consolidated force of their own.

Conversely, management is keenly aware of how powerful the unions have become and believe that any show of compassion on their part will be perceived by labor as a display of weakness. They entertain the delusion that the only thing labor will respect is more power. This stance results in the hardening of battle lines and a growing level of bitterness. The end result is a proliferation of strikes and the further crippling of business and industry.

Any mediator, whether of a contract dispute or a domestic quarrel, learns quickly that most parties of a dispute long for a harmonious settlement. Few people are pleased with unresolved conflict. Only the most maladjusted individuals enjoy adding fuel to the flames of controversy; only the morbid enjoy the pleasures of protracted hostility. Most people hunger for peace, but few are willing to pay the price for it.

For reconciliation to take place, someone must take the initial step away from the posture of hostility. We normally prefer, if not insist, that it be our opponent who does the moving. Our pride rapidly invades our conflicts, making it easier for the mediator to suggest movement than for us to take the step. This is one reason mediators become so unpopular, as each party in the conflict woos the mediator to side with him. If the mediator holds his place on neutral ground he risks the fury of both sides.

PEACEMAKING

The role of the mediator is also that of peacemaker. To engage in this activity is to share in the benediction pronounced by Christ on all who take such a responsibility seriously: "Blessed are the peacemakers, for they shall be called sons of God" (Matt. 5:9, *RSV*). The business of peacemaking is a task that should be common to the members of God's family.

The quest for peace was a passion of the Old Testament Jew. So profound was the national longing for peace that the very word became a daily expression of greeting and farewell. When a Jew meets another Jew, they exchange the salutation, *Shalom*. When the two part company, the word is not "good-bye" but once again the benediction of peace, *Shalom*. The national history of these people who have rarely enjoyed a *Pax Israelia* ingrains in them a wistful craving for peace.

Peace with God: Divine Peace

Peace was the most priceless legacy of Christ. He had no worldly goods to leave His disciples in His last will and testament. Only hours before His death, He said to them, "Peace I leave with you, my peace I give unto you: not as the world giveth, give I unto you" (John 14:27, *KJV*).

The peace Christ left behind was a transcendent peace, a sort not achieved by earthly remedies. It is a peace that eclipses human understanding, a quality that erases the restlessness of which Augustine spoke.

In biblical terms, peace is the firstfruit of one's reconciliation to God. Paul tells us, "Therefore being justified...we have peace with God" (Rom. 5:1, *KJV*).

What kind of peace is it that flows from justification?

The divine peace is a solid peace, a peace that is sustained with permanency. Once God reconciles a person to Himself, He does not adopt a posture of belligerence, poised to strike the instant we step out of line. We hear no sword-rattling with each transgression. Once we are reconciled to God, the estrangement is over, the hostilities have ended and the peace is sealed for eternity.

Peace on Earth: Fragile Peace

In this world the peace we enjoy is a fragile peace. A lasting memory from my childhood involves an incident that occurred on the streets of Chicago. Every day, my playmates and I joined together for a stickball game. The rules were defined by how far one could hit the ball, measured by the distance of manhole covers.

A ball struck past one sewer lid was a single, past two a double, and so on. Each child waited eagerly for his turn at bat. The magic moment came for me, and I was poised, waiting for the pitch, when a spontaneous clamor broke out around us, disrupting the game and leaving me on the verge of tears.

Adults were rushing around madly, behaving as if everyone had gone insane. People were yelling and dancing in the streets and beating spoons on metal dishpans. I was confused by the melee and rushed to my mother, begging for an explanation.

She hugged me and alternately laughed and cried, as tears of joy rushed down her cheeks. "It's over, it's over," she kept shouting.

Slowly, the meaning of it dawned on me. This was VJ Day 1945. It meant the war was over and my father was coming home. We could take the star-studded banner out of the window and become a family again.

That was my first experience of a wartime truce, an occasion of delirious joy. But then came the subsequent frightening drills in school as we were instructed in what to do in the event of an atomic attack. The hot war was over but its tenuous character was felt in the frigid moments of the cold war.

I was still a boy when another member of my family was shipped to Korea and was critically wounded by the blast of a mortar shell. When that conflict ended in truce, I was less optimistic about its enduring power.

I learned early that peace in this world is always tenuous at best. It stands in marked contrast to the peace treaty offered by God in His act of reconciliation.

Peace Without Repentance: False Peace
With every genuine article of value, there is the inevitable counterfeit. The Bible warns against the gossamer fabric of false peace. For people can be duped into a fraudulent security when peace has not yet come.

The lull before the storm can entice the thought that war has passed when the battle is ready to break. This kind of peace was the favorite promise of the false prophets of Israel. It is what Martin Luther called a "carnal peace."

While divinely appointed messengers, like Jeremiah, were delivering their oracles of doom, entreating the people to turn from their disobedient ways, the false prophets were prospering. Theirs was a more popular message as they, with the rhetoric of the demagogue, promised security to the people. Their vacuous promise provoked a feeling of peace backed by no substance in reality.

Jeremiah lamented the impact of these men. "For they have healed the hurt of the daughter of my people slightly, saying, Peace, peace; when there is no peace" (Jer. 8:11, *KJV*).

Jeremiah understood there could be no peace without repentance, no healing without the searing pain of the cauterization of the wound. The false prophets offered a placebo, a sugar pill to hide the taste of bile in the mouths of those estranged from their God. It is what the theologians call "cheap grace," what the statesmen call "peace without honor."

Authentic Peace: Achievable Peace

Identify the Problems to Be Solved. False peace occurs when the roots of estrangement are bypassed in favor of a superficial treatment of the problem. For authentic peace to take place, the real points of estrangement must be confronted. Before problems can be solved they must first be accurately identified.

Focus on the Feelings Expressed. We must be careful to take note of the feelings that are expressed. In marriage counseling, a common chore is to listen as couples argue about what is wrong in their marriage. The husband, for example, may complain bitterly that his wife does not love him. She, in turn, protests that her love is profound, complaining that he has no right to feel the way he does.

Getting to the truth of the matter requires the wisdom of Solomon and the patience of Job. Yet there is a shortcut to reconciliation. Without ever penetrating the ultimate accuracy of the circumstances, one can cut the Gordian knot[6] and work at the feeling level.

The counselor may offer the following observation: "It may be true that you love your husband. It may also be true that your husband has no right to feel that he is not loved. But one fact stands out clearly—his feelings are real. He honestly thinks that you do not love him, and that is the relevant fact we must deal with.

"Conversely, you are convinced that you do love him. You feel strongly about the matter and you think you have adequately demonstrated that love. Your husband may not think the demonstration is sufficient, but he must reckon with the obvious fact that you do believe that it is."

Direct Discussion Away from Who Is Right. By isolating

the feelings that are present, the discussion can be directed away from the Solomonic task of discerning who is ultimately right. Attention is focused on the feelings that are really present, leaving the ultimate vindication to the omniscient mind of God.

Recognize That Some People Enjoy a Fight. We have already noted that most people yearn for peace and the resolution of conflict. While it is true with respect to their own conflicts, it is not always true regarding other people's conflicts. There is a sense in which we love a fight.

We will pay large sums to watch professional fighters pummel each other in the ring. We join in the frenzy of the bench-clearing brawls in a hockey game, feeling a vicarious thrill when the "gloves come off." We take secret delight in hearing of another couple's domestic difficulties and, under the guise of "concern," relay the information to as many people as possible.

The fight is exciting and breaks the tedious monotony of our daily lives. The domestic quarrel is delicious fodder for the inveterate gossip who gets a distorted thrill out of broadcasting other people's difficulties. Perhaps it is nothing more than our human insecurity that we enjoy pointing to the warts on other people's noses, to make our own blemishes seem less pronounced.

Anticipate Resistance. The mediator will meet resistance in his role. The mediator must live in the full knowledge that his efforts toward reconciliation may be resisted not only by the estranged parties, but also by those who take delight in the continuation of the conflict.

Accept the Mandate to Work for Reconciliation. Because reconciliation can be painful, and attempts to achieve it often meet with great resistance, we may be tempted to despair of the task and leave it undone. But that is not an option for the Christian. The Christian is under a mandate to work for reconciliation.

"Therefore, if anyone is in Christ, he is a new creation; the old has gone, the new has come! All this is from God, who reconciled us to himself through Christ and gave us the ministry of reconciliation: that God was reconciling the world to himself in Christ, not counting men's sins against them. And he has committed to us the message of reconciliation. We are therefore Christ's ambassadors, as though God were making his appeal through us. We implore you on Christ's behalf: Be reconciled to God" (2 Cor. 5:17-20, *NIV*).

Some have drawn from this text the inference that reconciliation between God and mankind is already a *fait accompli*. Since God "was reconciling the world to himself," does this not mean that the task has been done and already exists as an objective reality?

Is the Church's task simply to inform the world that it has already been reconciled? Is the problem simply that we are already reconciled but not yet aware of it? By no means.

Certainly the pivotal act of reconciliation has been accomplished. The Cross stands as a finished moment in history. God has made His move and the reality of the atonement stands as an objective fact.

But the objective work of Christ does not effect our reconciliation to God automatically. There remains the necessity of our subjective response to it. The imperative stands, "Be reconciled to God."

Thus, reconciliation to God is not only a privilege, but a duty. We are commanded to be reconciled to Him. But the mandate does not stop there.

As our estrangement has three levels to it, so must our reconciliation. It is a mockery of God to claim reconciliation with Him while at the same time refusing it to our brother (see 1 John 4:20,21). We are warned by Christ not to approach His altar while estranged from our brother (see Matt. 5:23,24).

Peace with Oneself: Total Reconciliation

When these other wounds have been healed, then we may proceed to be reconciled with ourselves with no inhibiting barriers. To be at peace with oneself is the final result of total reconciliation.

FOR FURTHER REFLECTION

1. How can God demand love as a duty?
2. What does it mean to "fall in love"?
3. Name some people who have a loyal, steadfast love for you. Name the people for whom you have had loyal love.
4. How do we use "worst-case analysis" in our relationships?
5. What is the difference between a loyal friend and a yes-man?
6. What does the Bible mean by a "love which covers a multitude of sins"?
7. How do you understand unconditional love?
8. Why is 1 Corinthians 13 such a popular chapter of the Bible?
9. What is the difference between trust and credulity? Between vindication and vengeance?
10. Where do you see the need for reconciliation?

CHAPTER THREE

OUR SEARCH FOR DIGNITY

C HARLES Dickens began *A Tale of Two Cities* with the immortal lines: "It was the best of times, it was the worst of times." These words sound like a contradiction, dissonant to the ear, harsh to the brain.

How could the times be both best and worst?

Dickens was not indulging in incoherent gibberish, but was using a sound technique to grab the reader's attention. He was using the *paradox*, the apparent contradiction which begs for resolution.

He was calling attention to life in industrialized England and describing the two cities of London and Paris. His tale was of times when two kinds of life were being lived: a life which was glorious for the wealthy and wretched for the poor like Oliver Twist and his pickpocket pal, the Artful Dodger.

But even before Charles Dickens ever picked up a pen, the French mathematician, philosopher and writer, Blaise Pascal, had made use of the paradox. For Pascal, it was not merely England, but man himself who is the crowning paradox of all creation. He said that we are, at the same time, the creatures of highest grandeur and lowest misery.[1]

The paradox is that we can think, an ability which is a two-edged sword. That we can contemplate ourselves is our grandeur. The misery comes when we contemplate a better life than we now enjoy and realize we are unable to make it happen.

We have just enough knowledge to escape the bliss of ignorance. Translated into daily realities this means that a person with enormous wealth can conceive of yet more wealth, power, prestige, health, fame—all these things can be increased or improved. But consider that person who commands such a vast amount of money, yet who suffers from ill health or grieves over the death of a loved one.

We are able to dream of a better life but are unable to fulfill that perfect dream in this world. Rich men weep and powerful men howl, especially at the side of a grave.

DIGNITY AND DEATH

Measuring the Value of Life

The value of life grows in magnitude when we stare death in the eye. Death is obscene, a grotesque contradiction to life. The contrast between the vibrancy of a child at play and the limp, rag-doll look of a corpse is revolting. The cosmetic art of the mortician cannot disguise the odious face of death. The death of a friend or loved one robs us of a cherished companion and reminds us of our own mortality.

Death is no stranger to my household. I have hosted its unwelcome visit too many times. The two visits I recall most vividly are the times the black angel came for my parents. Both died at home—both deaths left trauma in my soul.

We chisel in stone the last words of epic heroes:

"I only regret that I have but one life to lose for my country," said Nathan Hale in 1776 before being hanged by the British as a spy.

"Oh my God," gasped John F. Kennedy, as he clutched his throat in a car in Dallas on a fateful Thursday in November 1963.

"Et tu, Brute,"[2] Caesar moaned, as he fell mortally wounded at the foot of Pompey's bust in the Roman Forum.

I remember my father's final words—how can I forget them? But what haunts me are my last words to him.

Death often leaves a burden of guilt to the survivors who are plagued by memories of things left unsaid or undone or of hurts imposed on the deceased. My guilt resides in the insensitive, nay, the stupid words I said to my father. I said the wrong thing, the juvenile thing for which death gave me no opportunity to say, "I'm sorry."

I long for the chance to replay the scene, but it is too late. I must trust the power of heaven to heal the wound. What is done can be forgiven—it can be augmented, diminished and, in some cases, repaired. But it cannot be undone.

Certain things cannot be recalled: the speeding bullet from the gun, the arrow released from the bow, the word that escapes our lips. We can pray that the bullet misses or that the arrow falls harmlessly to the ground, but we cannot command them to return in midflight.

What did I say that makes me curse my tongue? They were not words of rebellion or shouts of temper; they were words of denial—a refusal to accept my father's final statement. I simply said, "Don't say that, Dad."

In his final moments my father tried to leave me with a legacy to live by. He sought to overcome his own agony by encouraging me. He was heroic; I shrank from his words in cowardice. I could not face what he had to face.

I pled ignorance as I only understood enough of his words to recoil from them. He said, "Son, I have fought the good fight, I have finished the race, I have kept the faith."

He was quoting the apostle Paul's closing words to his

beloved disciple Timothy (2 Tim. 4:7, *RSV*). But I failed to recognize that fact. I had never read the Bible—I had no faith to keep, no race to finish.

My father was speaking from a posture of victory. He knew who he was and where he was going. But all I could hear in those words was that he was going to die.

What impertinence for me to reply, "Don't say that!" I rebuked my father in the most valiant moment of his life. I tramped on his soul with my own unbelief.

Nothing more was said between us—ever. I put his paralyzed arms around my neck, hoisting his useless body partially off the ground, supporting him on my back and shoulders, and dragged him to his bed. I left his room and shifted my thought to my homework assignments.

An hour later my studies were interrupted by the sound of a crash from a distant part of the house. I hastened to investigate the sound. I found my father sprawled in a heap on the floor with blood trickling from his ear and nose.

He lingered a day and a half in a coma before the rattle of death signaled the end. When his labored breathing stopped I leaned over and kissed his forehead.

I did not cry. I played the man, being outwardly calm through the following days of funeral home visitations and burial in the grave. But inside, I was devastated.

How much value did my father have to me then? I would have done anything I could, given everything I had, to bring him back. I had never tasted defeat so final or lost anything so precious. That was 34 years ago, but it does not require a psychiatrist to recognize that I am not over it yet.

My mother's death was different. Her death was tranquil, as she gained the exit from this world we all covet. She died in her sleep without a struggle.

Her last words to me were joyful. She said, moments before retiring to bed, "This is the happiest day of my life!"

She had lived a widow for nine years after losing her husband. Being a career woman she continued her work, investing her future joy in her children and grandchildren. Our first child was a daughter, bringing countless hours of delight to her grandmother.

My mother had two future goals she yearned to reach. She wanted to see my ordination to the ministry and she wanted a grandson who would carry on the family name, as I was the last surviving male of the Sproul side of the family.

My mother embarrassed me more than once with the pride she displayed about these passions. She would introduce me to her friends by saying, "My son is going into the ministry." No Jewish matriarch was ever more proud.

The family name was almost a fetish. I had been christened R.C. Sproul III. I almost wish she would have named me "Sue,"[3] both for all the teasing I endured from my peers about that Roman numeral and for all the scatological puns that the monicker "The third" can yield.

Mother made me promise that the tradition would live on, if my marriage produced a son. It was nonnegotiable; he had to be called R.C. IV. I was not sure whether I was trying to sire a son or to continue a dynasty, but who can refuse a widowed mother's pleas?

What made my mother's last day on earth so happy was the converging of dreams into one single day of glorious realization. While she was applying her makeup in preparation for going to work, I was pacing the floor of the expectant fathers' waiting room in a hospital 12 miles away. I had been there before but still did not feel like a confident veteran.

The same man who delivered our daughter finally came to the waiting room, with green mask dangling from his neck, to announce the birth of our son. My wife was fine and the dynasty was intact. After sharing the most tender of moments with my wife in the recovery room, I hurried to the phone to relay the news to my mother.

Nothing would do but that my mother would go to the hospital to see her new grandson. I picked her up at her office and took her to the hospital nursery to see the orange-haired, prune-faced newborn infant she declared uncommonly handsome. After a leisurely dinner at a restaurant, during which she expressed her unbounded ebullience, we went to her apartment where I was invited to spend the night.

As we reached the entrance to the building, we found two packages stacked against the doorway. Once inside the apartment, she tore open the packages like a child on Christmas morning. The first package contained engraved invitations to my ordination scheduled only weeks away.

The second package was from Maxine's, a stylish women's dress shop in Pittsburgh which featured the latest fashions. It contained an elegant dress, undoubtedly the most expensive garment she had purchased since her husband's death. She danced before the mirror holding the dress in front of her, taking waltz steps around the room.

She bought it for the ordination but wore it at her funeral. It was too much excitement for one day as one dream was fully realized and the other's proximate certainty was confirmed by the symbolic presence of the invitations and the dress. Within the hour she protested that she was weary and wanted to go to bed.

We said our good-nights and she retired to her bedroom, but not before poking her head around the door to say, "This is the happiest day of my life."

I was exhausted from the events of the day and quickly fell asleep in the next room. When morning came I knocked on my mother's door and was mildly puzzled by the lack of response. I opened the door and instantly realized that the woman in repose on the bed was dead.

It did not seem possible. I walked to her side and clutched

her wrist. She had been dead for several hours; rigor mortis had set in and her body was icy to the touch. The sensation was eerie, defying logic.

Sleep makes the passage of time seem instantaneous. In what seemed like the span of a few minutes, my mother had changed from a breathing, warm, excited person to a lifeless statue. I stood transfixed in disbelief, caught in the absurdity of it. Within the span of 24 hours, I passed through the emotions of seeing my son take his initial breaths of life and seeing my mother in the coldness of death.

Questioning the Meaning of Life

Moments like these carve themselves in the memory bank of the mind. Life goes on as the world continues to turn. We push those memories to the deepest recesses of the brain, hoping they will lose their piercing torment with the passing of time. But they are always there to nag us with the question of the meaning of life.

When death intrudes it is easy to succumb to the seductive call of despair. Shakespeare's tragic heroes courted it and some even embraced it. Drawing from his intimate knowledge as playwright and poet, Shakespeare in *Macbeth* used the image of the aspiring actor to dramatize his point:

> Out, out, brief candle!
> Life's but a walking shadow, a poor player
> That struts and frets his hour upon the stage,
> And then is heard no more; it is a tale
> Told by an idiot, full of sound and fury,
> Signifying nothing.[4]

The young thespian dreams of the day he will graduate from bit parts to a leading role. The magic audition happens and he begins to prepare for his big opportunity. He pours himself into the role, studying his character and memorizing his lines. He rehearses until each word is expressed with the correct inflection and each gesture is delivered with a timely flair.

Opening night finally arrives and the actor's stomach churns as he fidgets in his dressing room while attendants apply grease-paint to his face. His heart leaps to his throat when the ominous knock comes at the door, alerting him that the curtain is about to rise. The actor moves to the wings, peering on stage at the scenery, arranged and waiting for his entrance.

On cue, he plunges into the light, taking his place on center stage. He feels the heat emanating from the footlights; their glare blinds his eyes to the mass of people watching his every move. He blanks the audience from his mind as he concentrates on merging into the character he must portray. He is caught up in the flow of the drama until the climax swells to its passionate conclusion.

As the curtain falls, the audience is on its feet, cheering wildly, demanding one more glimpse of the triumphant actor. He steps to center stage to take his bow. It is a moment of ecstasy as he is engulfed by waves of applause.

He wants to freeze this moment forever, but the clock will not allow it. The clapping dies down and people make their way out of the theater. That night the sleep of the actor is sweet as he revels in his glory.

But all glory must fade. Twenty years later, the actor is left with a yellowed press notice, and the mention of his night as the answer to a trivia question. The work, the passion and the striving are snuffed out like a candle.

Shakespeare says life is like that and like listening to a story from a moron, a babbling idiot. Lots of noise, but no meaning.

Who doesn't feel like that at times?

The black slave felt helpless before his never-ending labor. He likened it to the ceaseless movement of "Ol' Man River." It was always and ever:

Tote that barge. Lift that bale.
Get a little drunk and you land in jail.

We recall his final statement:

I gets weary and tired of tryin';
I'm tired of livin' and scared of dyin'.*

This expression is not as eloquent as Hamlet's soliloquy, "To Be or not to Be," but the sentiment is the same.

When the burning candle reaches the end of the taper the idiot's tale is terrifying. Sound and fury with no meaning is more than any person can stand. That life should add up to an empty zero elicits a scream from the marrow of the bones.

The poetry of Shakespeare dwarfs our inarticulate moans; but the cry is the same—it is the universal groan of man aching for dignity.

DIGNITY AND HUMAN "PROGRESS"

The moral issue of human dignity has become a consuming problem in our day. So crucial is the question that we sometimes wonder if man's "progress" into the twentieth century—and soon into the twenty-first century—is a vast unconscionable mistake. How did we move from the optimism of the Declaration of Independence to the brink of annihilation in a little more than 200 years?

False Assumptions
Our republic's beginning came on the heels of a political and scientific revolution which swept Western civilization. It came in the midst of a time period we call the Age of Enlightenment.[5] The

*"OL' MAN RIVER" (From "SHOW BOAT"). Words by Oscar Hammerstein II. Music by Jerome Kern. Copyright © 1927 PolyGram International Publishing, Inc. Copyright

Enlightenment was complex, but one of its central motifs was that *the God-hypothesis was no longer needed to explain the origin of man and his world.*

Men like the French Baron D'Holbach,[6] who described himself as "the personal enemy of God," took refuge in the idea of "spontaneous generation" to explain the origin of man and the world. This view, though later repudiated as being repugnant to science, was greeted by many with enthusiastic response as some shouted, "Good riddance" to God.

False Optimism

The most obvious benefit of the exile of God was that man could "come of age" and be responsible for his own future. This was "liberation day" when men would no longer need to live in fear of the deity's awful revenge, nor have to rush to the church in supplicant penance, seeking the indulgence of her priests. Man was free from accountability to God.

Religious school was out and the pupils were joyously singing, "No more pencils, no more books, no more teacher's sassy looks." The bewhiskered God of Sinai, who thundered commandments combined with threats of everlasting torment for the disobedient, was wrestled from His throne. There would be no more making lists and checking them twice, to see who was being naughty and nice, save for the relegating of that task to Santa Claus.

No wonder the optimism. It was to be a brave new world with endless possibilities for human progress. The dawn of the nineteenth century brought an unprecedented spirit of optimism as modern man began to build his utopia.

The industrial revolution sparked rapid advances. The age-old problem of food production was solved; higher education came within the reach of the masses; monarchies crumbled as the grand experiment of democracy brought new freedom to the world.

Immigrants rushed to this country heading for the statue holding aloft a torch and inviting, "Give me your tired, your poor, your huddled masses yearning to breathe free."[7] Material wealth was produced which was thought impossible in all the centuries preceding it.

False Security

The golden age of optimism of the nineteenth century began to tarnish with the advent of the twentieth century and turned to rust with the modern invention of global war. World War I cast a shadow over the enlightened champions of limitless progress. Many, however, were undaunted by this brief throwback to primitive savagery, viewing it as the final vestigal remnant of mankind's adolescence, calling it simply, "The war to end all wars."[8]

Versailles[9] brought it all to a halt and renewed the hopeful spirit that would prevail all the way to Munich and Neville Chamberlain's classic pose as he leaned over a balcony, with an umbrella neatly perched on his forearm, proclaiming that he had achieved "peace for our time."[10]

Chamberlain's "peace" lasted for hours only as the Nazi blitzkrieg[11] was mobilized. World War II proved not to be the war to end all wars either, as the planet was jolted rudely into the nuclear age and the omega point began to look like a point of annihilation. The issue for man now is not so much utopia as survival.

THE DEATH OF DIGNITY?

As a college student in the late '50s, I was frightened by reading an essay in Humanities entitled "Man's Margin of Error." I no longer recall the author's name, nor could I quote verbatim from the text of the essay. The thesis of the brief study, however, remains indelibly stamped in my mind.

No Margin of Error—No Safety
The core idea was that man throughout history has worked with a certain safety margin for his errors. He could indulge himself with acts of violence and warfare and survive his own folly. But with the advent of nuclear arms, that safety margin has almost vanished. The margin has shrunk so far and so rapidly that no one knows where the fail-safe point is. Man carves out

---

Our anthropology is intimately bound up with our theology....If there is no divine glory, there is no human dignity.

---

his future as a race, daily intimidated by a nuclear sword of Damocles.[12]

The essay went on to detail the leap in man's capacity for self-destruction. It provided a calculus of destructive power found in various weapons of war. For example, if we compare the degree of destructive power of the primitive bow and arrow with the atomic bomb that was dropped on Hiroshima, we begin to see something of the "progress" of human ingenuity.

It required eons of time for man to advance from the bow and arrow to nuclear power. What is terrifying is that in the space of 14 years, from 1945-1959, the gap was bridged again. That is, the bombs developed by 1959 were as many times more powerful than the atomic bomb which fell on Hiroshima as the Hiroshima bomb was more powerful than the bow and arrow.

Who knows where the ratio stands today as the margin of error diminishes to the point of nothingness. We rush madly to what General Douglas MacArthur warned us of from the deck of the battleship *Missouri* on September 2, 1945 at the formal ceremony of Japanese surrender: Armageddon.

We see the future through a clouded glass. Perhaps tomorrow a new discovery will make atomic weapons obsolete and neutralized of any significance. Perhaps for the first time in human history man will invent destructive weapons but refrain from using them. Perhaps the balance of power will remain so delicate that atomic swords will be used for rattling only.

Perhaps.

But if one monstrous button is pushed, both man and his margin of error could be vaporized.

No Accountability—No Dignity

The price tag of our enlightenment has been steep. Perhaps it is true that man is not ultimately accountable. But if this is so, it should not occasion rejoicing, but mourning for the death of dignity.

If dignity is dead, then we must move with B. F. Skinner beyond freedom and dignity[13] to that new frontier where only slavery and indignity can dwell. We enter Skinner's world through Dante's gates of hell, blinking shut our eyes lest we read the awful warning sign, "Abandon hope, all ye who enter here."[14]

We refuse to abandon hope as we shrink from Dante's inferno. We are men, and it is a part of our character to nurture hope in our bosom. Our hope for dignity is both our blessing and our curse.

Every person who has ever played golf knows how stubborn hope can be, how difficult it is to destroy. Our spirits may sink and flirt with despair but one decent shot on the eighteenth hole is enough to make us ready to try it again.

The story is told of the frustrated golfer who, after enduring a humiliating round, walked off the last green and promptly threw his clubs, expensive bag and all, into a lake. He stormed off in a mixture of fury and dejection to the locker room. He walked straight to the shower room and in the privacy there, grasped a razor and slit both of his wrists.

Standing by the sink with his life blood pouring down the

drain, he heard his golfing comrades enter the locker room, shouting, "Hey, Dale, do you want to play again tomorrow?"

Dale quickly pressed his wrists tightly together and poked his head out around the door, saying, "What time?"

THE DEATH OF GOD

We remember Friedrich Nietzsche[15] who declared, "God is dead...he died of pity." His declaration of the death of God was not made in defiance, but in tears.

If God Is Dead, Life Has No Dignity

His work was distorted and abused by some who were captivated by it. Among them was a certain demented Bavarian paperhanger who sent copies of Nietzsche's books to his brownshirted friends as Christmas presents. Adolf Hitler's madness not only did nothing to advance the cause of human dignity, he left Europe in her darkest hour of indignity.

After pondering the death camps of Buchenwald and Auschwitz, Albert Camus[16] remarked that the only serious question left for philosophers to discuss is the question of suicide.

We recall the fad movement in religion known as the "Death of God" theology. One clever journalist responded by printing a mock poll of the reactions of public figures to the news of the deity's demise:

Said Dwight D. Eisenhower, "Gosh, I didn't know he was ill."

Said Billy Graham, "It can't be so, I talked to Him this morning."

Said Harry S Truman, "It's a damn shame."

Can we blame poor Nietzsche, who died in a lunatic asylum, for all this? Not really. Devotees of Nietzsche are quick to argue that applications of his ideas like those made by Adolf Hitler were severe distortions.

Where then was the fire that yielded the Nazi smoke?

If God Is Dead, Life Has No Meaning

Nietzsche examined man and his world and came to the depressing conclusion that life is meaningless, that man has no dignity. The final verdict is found in the words *"Das Nichtige"* (the nothingness). Nietzsche is claimed as the father of *nihilism*, the philosophy that declares there are no values, no meaning, no significance to life.

Nietzsche refused to surrender to despair, calling for the emergence of the "Superman" who would show us how to live in an absurd world. The Superman is bold and daring; he lives by courage, "Sailing his ship into uncharted seas and building his house on the slopes of Vesuvius."

The curse of the Superman, his fatal dose of Kryptonite, is found in the kind of courage he must have. Nietzsche called it "dialectical courage," meaning a type of courage that functions in the tension of certain failure. The sad plight of Superman is that he must value courage when he knows it is useless; he must seek significance knowing full well that he is insignificant.

If God Is Dead, Life Has No Victory

It is like Jimmy Cagney flying his crippled plane into the sheer rock face of the White Cliffs of Dover, spitting out the shattered cockpit window at the wall microseconds before he crashes in a fiery explosion. The audience shouts its approval of this defiant heroic gesture as the film fades to sunset and the house lights come on.

The imagination refuses to picture the morrow when the sun comes up and glistens once more from the chalky cliffs. The cliffs are impervious to the events of the day before, while the mangled body of the pilot lies trapped in the wreckage of the plane at the bottom of the sea, the defiant grin rigid in death. The cliffs win and Cagney loses, save for a brief moment of dialectical courage.

It is Ernest "Papa" Hemingway bringing his fictional characters to life by staging his own death.[17] The Hemingway hero assaults the sea, the ravages of war, the mountain of Kilimanjaro and the wild bull in the ring. He "grabs the bull by the horns" and determines his own destiny.

Hemingway said that the only edge we can gain over death is to determine for ourselves the time, the place and the method of dying. He penned these thoughts before he carefully orchestrated his own "victory" by blowing his brains out with his favorite hunting rifle.

Nietzsche's anguished life portrayed the futility of trying to live by dialectical courage. His own quest for dignity ended in the tragedy of insanity. He signed his last raving letters with the signature, "The Crucified One." His sister exploited the situation by selling tickets to a curious public who would pay money to get a glimpse of her famous deranged brother.

If God Is Dead, Then Man Is Too

Our anthropology is intimately bound up with our theology. If God is exiled, so is man; if God is dead, man is too. If we are not accountable, then we do not count.

If there is no divine glory, there is no human dignity. We can try to have one without the other, but to do so is to genuflect to the lunacy of intellectual schizophrenia.

DIGNITY AND HUMAN ORIGINS

We become cynical when we remember the carnival atmosphere of the celebrated Scopes "monkey trial" in Tennessee.[18] Religion gets a black eye when the newspapers sensationalize the court battles in Arkansas and elsewhere waged over the issue of creation versus evolution in the schoolroom.

Why so much fuss?

The Issue of Human Dignity

We need to understand that the issues are deeper than questions of church and state and arguments about theology and biology. The central issue which fuels the controversy is the issue of human dignity.

Sometimes television marketing specialists and demographers are surprised by public reaction. The textbook case of marketing shock came with the overwhelmingly popular response to television miniseries "Roots," based on Alex Haley's book of the same title published in 1976. The charts were smashed and the Nielsen ratings blitzed by viewer reaction.

How do we account for that? The acting was superb as we were caught up in the heroic struggle of the enslaved African, Kunte Kinte, and the personality of Chicken George. Yet the public reaction to "Roots" is impossible to explain, simply in terms of quality acting and a moving story line.

And this was more than white America flagellating itself for the sins of its fathers. Most of us are weary of the guilt trip and would appreciate respite from it. We do not need to stay glued to the television set for each episode of "Roots" to torture ourselves for our sins of prejudice.

"Roots" was far more than a racial statement. Haley captured the heart of every man and woman who cares about human dignity. He stated that the years of research he poured into tracing his own ancestry were motivated by his personal quest for dignity.

Alex Haley had to know where he came from. He sought out his origins. He was searching for his roots.

The Question of Ultimate Origin

But the search goes beyond the third or fourth generation. It is not enough for the white man to know that one of his forefathers came over on the *Mayflower* or for Haley to know that his ancestors arrived in Virginia on the slave ship named *Lord Ligonier*. We must push the question back further into time.

Where did our ancestors' ancestors come from? Somewhere the genealogy stops for all of us as we meet at the lower tip of the root. The question of our ultimate root, our ultimate origin, is what makes the monkey trial so hotly disputed.

When we consider human dignity we cannot ignore questions of origin and destiny, as our past and our future define our present. There is no such thing as *the* theory of evolution. Many different theories abound, ranging from simple matters of growth, change and adaptation of a species created in the image of God, to the more radical sort which argues that man began as an accident, emerging from the slime by some mysterious process with no abiding purpose.

The latter suggestion is a bitter pill to swallow, and one need not be a philosopher to feel the weight of its implications. If I come from nothing and I end in nothing, how can I have real value now?

The irony is that the question of human origin is not, in the final analysis, a biological question. Biology can shed light on the guesswork about human beginnings but it is ultimately a question of history at its dawn. One philosopher described our dilemma this way: "Man is a grown-up germ, sitting on one cog of one wheel of a vast cosmic machine that is slowly, but inexorably running down to nothingness."

If we are told we are merely sophisticated germs, inchoate blobs of protoplasm, then it is no wonder we yell for religion or alcohol or drugs or anything else that might still the tempest of our souls. We will do anything to flee the verdict that we are worthless.

We are like the atheist who was climbing a mountain when he stumbled and slipped over a precipice only to begin dropping sharply through 14,000 feet of space. He managed to break his fall, at least momentarily, by grabbing onto a spindly twig growing feebly out of the side of the mountain.

Suspended in air, one hand clutching the branch which was starting to break loose from its moorings, he looked to heaven and cried out in desperation, "Is there anyone up there who can help me?"

A rich baritone voice pierced the clouds: "I am God. I will help you. Just show me your faith by letting go of the branch."

The climber looked down to the ravine beneath him, then up to the heavens and cried once more, "Is there anybody *else* up there who can help me?"

Our Theological Conviction
Human dignity is built on the conviction that someone is up there who can help us. Behind human dignity is a theology that cannot be minimized.

I was addressing the top executives of a Fortune 500 corporation. It was a small group composed of regional vice-presidents and the president and chairman of the board. The surroundings were plush with the teak panels artfully creating an ambience of power and prestige. The patrician audience was a bit nervous about my mixing "religion" and business as I spoke.

When the seminar was near completion the chairman of the board became excited as his eyes lit up in understanding. "Let me see if I can connect what you're saying. What I hear is that our business life is affected by how we treat people. How we treat people is a matter of ethics. Ethics are determined by our philosophy. Our philosophy reflects our theology—so respecting people is really a theological matter."

In simple terms, the chairman was expressing what Dostoevski[19] meant when he said, "If there is no God, all things are permissible," or what Sartre[20] was driving at when he said, "Man is a useless passion." These are statements about human dignity and they touch the auto worker, the coal miner, the newspaper reporter and the insurance salesman. If nobody is at home in heaven, then the labor of the corporate executive and the labor of the janitor are equally useless.

The Humanist Contradiction

Some seek to sidestep the dilemma by skirting the issues with the artful dodge of compromise. The humanist rejects God while affirming loudly the value of people. He joins hands with Christians and Jews to march for human rights, to eliminate slavery,

---

Man's dignity rests in God who assigns an inestimable worth to every person.

---

to halt the oppression of the poor, to build hospitals that care for men and women in misery. He exalts the virtues of honesty, justice, compassion, but he must crucify his mind to do it.

For the humanist is caught in the vicious contradiction of ascribing dignity to creatures who live their lives between the poles of meaninglessness. He lives on borrowed capital, deriving his values from the Judeo-Christian faith, while at the same time repudiating the very foundation upon which these values rest. He is still looking for someone else up there to help him, but no answer comes. His assigning of value to man is utterly gratuitous, based not on reason but on preference and preference alone.

We must ask the humanist some harsh and difficult questions: Why should we care at all about the plight of insignificant grown-up germs? What difference does it make if the white germs subjugate the black germs and make them sit at the back of the bus? Who cares if meaningless blobs of protoplasm are exploited in a steel mill or robbed in the halls of justice?

Oh, you say, the black germs care and the little blobs of protoplasm cry out.

Again, I say, "So what?" A creature with no ultimate value, one who is ultimately insignificant is not worth any sacrifice. Tell it to the idiot, as he alone can live with empty sound and fury. If man is valueless, then we can all sleep in tomorrow morning.

Apart from hard-boiled skeptics, few of us respond to humanism in such fashion. We follow sentimentality and accept the humanist's happy inconsistency. We too are human and are often content to let the humanist retain the cake he has already eaten.

We applaud his magic feat of having a world come from nothing, like the rabbit out of the hat. We stare in wonder at his ability to get being from nothingness, dignity from insignificance, personality from impersonality; and we marvel at the humanist's ability to stand firmly with both feet planted in midair.

A Christian Worldview

On the other hand, our passion for human worth rests not on magic but on the sober basis of a Christian worldview. Man's dignity rests in God who assigns an inestimable worth to every person. Man's origin is not an accident, but a profoundly intelligent act by One who has eternal value; by One who stamps His own image on each person.

God creates men and moves heaven and earth to redeem them when they fall. Our origin is in creation and our destiny is for redemption. Between these points every human heartbeat has value.

The future of our race is not grim as long as a Creator-Redeemer runs the universe. We are not a lost planet wandering aimlessly in space; we are a visited planet with a glorious destiny.

It is easy to feel lost at times, cut off from our roots and blind to our future. There are times when we can identify with

Alice in Wonderland when she came to a fork in the road and knew not which way to turn. She too looked upward for help and found not God, but the grinning Cheshire Cat.

"Please, Mr. Cat, help me. Tell me which road I should take?"

"That depends," said the cat. "Where are you going?"

"I don't know," muttered the confused Alice.

"Then it doesn't matter...," said the fiendish cat.

DIGNITY AND SIN

There is a road to redemption where every human being has dignity. Many reject this road because they think Christianity destroys self-esteem, disparaging human value with woeful denunciations of the evil of man. Preachers rail against corruption, calling man a wretched sinner.

Did not David cry out, "I am a worm and not a man" (Ps. 22:6, *NIV*) and Job grovel in the dust, moaning, "I despise my life" (Job 7:16, *NIV*)?

God Takes Sin Seriously Because Mankind Has Value

These grim statements make it seem that Christianity has a low view of human dignity. But the point often overlooked is that the character of sinfulness in no way diminishes the worth of persons. It is because humanity is so valuable that God takes sin seriously.

We may be annoyed at the news that a rat has been eaten by a cat, but we are not morally outraged. We do not pity the poor rat or ask what the rat has done to deserve being consumed by the cat. But let a larger cat maul a human child and we are incensed.

When a fly is swatted or a whale slaughtered, some may protest, but none calls it a holocaust. Yet the whale knows nothing of sin, and the fly is ignorant of morality.

Mankind Has Value Because Man Bears the Image of God

These creatures are by no means valueless, but none of them bears the image of God. When men sin against men, personhood is violated. The quality of human life is assaulted by what we call sin.

People are hurt, deprived, exploited and made miserable by moral transgression. Hence we weep, for we are both victim and perpetrator of personal evil.

By taking sin seriously, we take man seriously. Evil may mar the divine image and cloud its brilliance, but it cannot destroy it. The image can be defaced, but it can never be erased. The most obscene symbol in human history is the Cross; yet in its ugliness it remains the most eloquent testimony to human dignity.

THE EXPERIENCE OF INDIGNITY

While doing research for the book *Stronger Than Steel*,[21] I was puzzled by an expression steelworkers used frequently to describe their experiences on the foundry floor. Noticeably, the black laborers resorted to this descriptive phrase, "The supervisor comes in and he drops his head."

I was not certain what the "dropping his head" expression meant until I was involved in a seminar at a hospital. Walking through the corridors of the hospital to observe the dynamics of the local scene, I paid particular attention to the nurses as they performed their tasks on the floor. As a silent observer, I tuned in to their nonverbal communication.

The Doctor Acknowledged

One pattern became quickly evident. When a doctor entered the area there was a noticeable change in the nurses' demeanor. The pace became more brisk, the posture more upright and the bearing more alert. As the doctor drew near, even the classic gestures of feminine preening became manifest. The doctor's presence was clearly noted, even without words being exchanged.

Shortly after the departure of the doctor, I watched as one of the nurses, who had so obviously preened, made her way down a corridor. Coming down the hall from the other direction was a man pushing a cart filled with soiled laundry. The man represented the pariah, the lower caste of the housekeeping department.

The Worker Ignored

As he beheld the nurse, he raised his head to a position of acknowledgment, and his face brightened in anticipation of a greeting. At virtually the same instant, the nurse tilted her head downward and focused her eyes on the floor as she moved curtly past the man. The man's face darkened in disappointment as the brightness vanished from his eyes. His pace became noticeably slower as he shuffled down the hall.

What had transpired in microseconds was probably not a matter of conscious realization by either party in the nonverbal transaction, but it clearly took place. As I witnessed the byplay, it dawned on me exactly what the laborers in the mill were talking about. The nurse had "dropped her head" as an outward sign of refusing to acknowledge the presence of another human being.

The housekeeping worker was made to feel invisible, as if he did not exist. For him, that incident was an experience of indignity. When that kind of "minor" indignity is repeated countless times a day, strong feelings of hostility arise, not surprisingly, between groups of different status and prestige levels.

THE NATURE OF DIGNITY

What then is dignity?

Dignity has been a major issue in our culture for years. Black people understand the issue. The Jewish people have majored in the problem.

From the days of antiquity, the Jewish nation has struggled with the question of dignity. As a race of people, they have been subjected to calculated genocide. The extreme degree to which the Holocaust exhibited anti-Semitism cannot be understood as a spontaneous interlude perpetuated by an insane few in a brief time warp of history.

The pogrom and the ghetto are established historical methods of dealing with the Jew. From Pharaoh to Nebuchadnezzar, from Masada[22] to Warsaw,[23] the wandering Jew has been a principal target of the atrocity of indignity. Adolf Eichmann[24] was still a teenager when Harold Abrahams punished his lungs in his 100-meter dash for dignity in the 1924 Paris Olympics.[25]

Dignity Is Rooted in Glory
The idea of dignity is rooted in the Old Testament concept of *glory*. In the created realm, all things reflect some degree of this glory. The stars have a certain glory, as do the moon and the sun. There is a glory ascribed to fish, fowl and the beasts of the field; a glory to the man and a glory to the woman.

Glory Is an Attribute of God
Ultimately glory derives from an attribute of God Himself. It is the heavenly glory of God that defines the essence of glory. The usual translation of the biblical concept of glory into Latin is the simple *gloria*. There are instances when another Latin word is chosen, the term *dignitas*, which mirrors the link between our word *dignity* and the Hebrew concept of glory.

The ancient Jews were not abstract in their thinking: They liked to speak in concrete images and had a love for the figurative and metaphorical. So we uncover a clue to the original meaning of glory by looking at its Hebrew root. The word "glory" comes from the Hebrew word for "weightiness."

When they ascribed glory to God they were saying that God was "weighty" or "heavy." Yet they did not conceive of God as a grossly-overweight or obese deity in the sky. God was not considered weighty in pounds, but in significance.

God was conceived as having substantial or "solid" existence. There is a permanence associated with God which no creature possesses.

In contrast, man is pictured in ephemeral terms, the fragility of his life likened to grass. We are told, "All men are like grass, and...the grass withers" (1 Pet. 1:24, *NIV*). The ungodly man is described in even more transient terms; he is as "the chaff which the wind driveth away" (Ps. 1:4, *KJV*), having no weight, no substance.

The idea that dignity is tied to heaviness is not foreign to English-speaking people. We express the same notion in our informal patterns of speech. Consider the college student's response to a profound lecture by one of his professors. The student mutters, "Heavy," as he ponders the points of the lecture.

In another context, the student might respond by saying, "He laid a heavy trip on us."

Conversely when we feel we are being unduly ignored or not taken seriously we complain, "That person took me lightly." To be taken lightly is to be treated with indignity, to be deemed insignificant. Here one's value or worth as a person is called into question.

Man's Glory Is Derived from God
We have already seen the close link between dignity and worth. It is because God has assigned worth to man and woman that human dignity is established. Man's glory is derived; he is dependent upon God's glory for his own.

Man enjoys such an exalted rank in the nature of things because mankind bears the image of God. From his creation to his redemption, man's dignity is preserved. He is created by

One who is eternal and is made for a redemption which stretches into eternity.

His origin is significant—his destiny is significant—he is significant.

FOR FURTHER REFLECTION

1. Write your own definition of "dignity."
2. How do you feel your sense of dignity is undermined?
3. How is human dignity related to creation?
4. How does accountability relate to man's worth?
5. Why do African-Americans and Jews care so much about dignity?
6. How do you react to the "victory" of Hemingway's suicide?
7. Why do people think Christianity has a low view of man?
8. Where does man's power of being come from?
9. How do you respond to the idea that "man is the measure of all things"?
10. Why do we have a crisis of human dignity in our day?

CHAPTER FOUR

DIGNITY IN THE HOME

HUMAN dignity begins in the home. The family is the breeding ground of all interpersonal relationships; the basic sociological unit where personal character is first molded and self-identity first formed.

If the child is not valued in the home, it is difficult for him to gain a sense of self-worth anywhere else. If he feels worthless himself, it is hard for him to impart a sense of dignity to people he meets outside the home, for he cannot give away what he does not first possess himself.

So we can speak of the home as the cradle of human worth where love and respect must be carefully nurtured and jealously guarded.

DIGNITY AND MARRIAGE

If the family is the atomic unit of society, its nucleus is found in the husband/wife relationship. The mood of the marriage creates the atmosphere in which children are reared. The atmosphere may tingle with the promise of the freshness of a spring day, the kind of air that makes one eager for the future. Or the atmosphere may be heavy with storm clouds of anger or oppressive with the muggy smog which smothers the breath and leaves grimy stains on the soul.

A child enjoys seeing the playful hug, the good-bye kiss and the spontaneous frolic of parents in love. Though young, children are acutely aware of the threat of divorce to the security of their homes. They tune in to the soap operas and the tears of their classmates who have already been casualties.

They wince when the sounds of parental fights assault their ears and they feel pain in their stomachs when they witness quarrels. For the child to acquire an elementary understanding of love, he must see a mature model of it in his parents. If the child grows up in a combat zone, sees too much fighting, hears too many insults, the flowering of his own capacity for love is stunted by a killing frost.

The Anticipation of a Happy Marriage

Few couples enter marriage with the intent of dissolving it in divorce at a later date. Some have married for the convenience of tax benefits, for the advantage of welfare subsidies or with a devious view toward a lucrative alimony settlement.

But Cinderella is not yet dead, and young women still stand before their windows singing, "A dream is a wish your heart makes...." The anticipation of marriage remains an exciting joy in itself, a time when people savor each step of preparation for the wedding.

I thought my interest in domestic utensils ended when "the dish ran away with the spoon" and I graduated from nursery rhymes. But spoons and dishes became romantic once more when I went with my fiancee to choose china and a silver pattern. The planning was fun with the renting of tuxedos, the ordering of flowers and the selection of a cake.

My bride was ecstatic when her parents accompanied her to the bridal shop to choose the gown of a lifetime. She had a hope chest, aptly named because it contained those things in which her future hope was symbolically invested. Most couples share the dream that will yield the "happily ever after" conclusion.

Memories of the wedding day cling to the brain cells. Few things stimulate my capacity for nostalgia or my penchant for the sentimental more than memories of those hours. Certain moments stand out as vivid vignettes of the occasion:

> I remember shaving, ever so carefully—examining the mirror for the stray whisker I missed and avoiding scrupulously the nick that would blemish my countenance.
>
> I remember applying black shoe polish to the soles of my shoes so they would not glare at the congregation when we knelt for the minister's blessing.
>
> I remember standing in the corridor adjacent to the sanctuary, pacing back and forth like a caged panther while my best man tried in vain to settle me down.
>
> I remember synchronizing my watch with the minister's so I would know the precise second to walk through the door and move to the chancel steps.
>
> I remember blushing when my smiles broke too wide as I watched the bridesmaids proceed down the aisle.

Far in the back of the church I could make out the silhouette of my bride holding on to her father's arm, awaiting the strains of the bridal march. My eyes flooded as the congregation rose to signal the grand entrance of my woman. She came step by step, walking with regal delicacy over the immaculate linen runner, finally reaching my side.

The ceremony seemed to move with blinding speed, with the pledging of our troth and the making of our vows over too quickly. I looked Vesta in the eye as I recited my vows with an intensity that filled the church. I felt the pressure of the minister's hands on my head as he consecrated our vows with prayer.

Then came the dynamic moment when the organ burst forth, with full diapason, into the triumphant sounds of Henry Purcell's

---

Selfless love is as remote from the biblical view of love as Star Wars *is from* Gone with the Wind.

"Trumpet Voluntary." In our joyous recessional, I stumbled clumsily, tangling my feet in the silk organza covering the hoop of my wife's gown. The congregation chuckled in delight, as I blushed once more when Vesta started our marriage by offering me her steady hand, a harbinger of things to come.

We waltzed through the narthex and made our way to the reception hall where we stood for hours, shaking hands with friends and relatives. Those moments were the darkest of the day; the receiving line seemed to last forever, with my ill-fitting shoes agonizingly pinching my toes and an injudiciously placed fern needling my posterior. But the darkness lifted with our cutting of the cake and the uninhibited mischief of shoving cake into each other's mouth.

Our wedding day was unforgettable; a day experienced in similar fashion by millions of couples whose hearts overflow with future expectations.

The Heartbreak of a Severed Union

So what happens to break the spell and cast the pieces of the broken dream into the ash heap of the divorce court? The happy memory of my own wedding day is marred by the knowledge that of the five men who stood by my side that day, four are divorced and the fifth is in the legal process of finalizing his divorce.

Why this epidemic of broken marriages? Why the heartbreak of severed unions?

Conflict invades the bliss of marriage and forces the adjustment of expectations downward. When the expected joys of marriage fail to materialize, disappointment and frustration intrude, with anger in their wake. Romance turns to warfare as the anger escalates.

Psychologists and professional counselors have isolated the major problem areas that emerge in marriage. The most frequent problems include conflict in sexual adjustment, financial matters, in-law relations and role expectations.

SEXUAL DIGNITY

The sexual relationship is the most volatile of all human relationships, touching people at their deepest level of vulnerability. In the act of sex, we are stripped to complete nakedness, going beyond the physical to the emotional and psychological. In sex, we are "uncovered" and exposed.

Let a man be eminently successful in his business career, and he will feel like a miserable failure if he is impotent with his wife. Let a woman be the social paragon of the community, and she will feel worthless if her sexual relationship with her husband is a disaster. If this area of the marriage falters, the relationship is strained, and the fragile human ego is assailed by doubt.

Mutual Fulfillment
Much has been written, particularly by Christian authors, of the need for selfless love in marriage and in the marriage bed. We

are exhorted to care for the needs of our spouse without concern for our own fulfillment. The nuptial vow, we are told, binds us to a pledge of selfless giving to our partners.

Nonsense. Selfless love and lovemaking is as remote from the biblical view of love as *Star Wars* is from *Gone with the Wind.*

Varieties of Eastern religion pursue the goal of losing one's self-identity into the "one" of the cosmos or of absorbing the self into some ethereal oversoul. The Christian, however, does not enter the bed chamber, chanting "oom."

The Bible nowhere advocates the annihilation of the self, but promotes the redemption of the self. The Bible rebukes selfish love, but nowhere does it advocate selfless love.

Imagine what it would be like to practice an utterly selfless kind of love. The self would be allowed no personal joy, no personal pleasure in the love relationship. As soon as the self enjoyed any sense of gratification, it would trigger a warning buzzer that the norm of selfless love had been violated.

Yet nothing is wrong with a person's relishing the act of lovemaking. Our Creator was not capricious in designing our anatomy with a concentration of nerve endings where they involuntarily excite feelings of pleasure during sex. To sublimate the natural physical delight by intent is to insult our Creator.

When I pursued marriage I did not set out to find a woman to whom I could give myself away entirely, sacrificing any hope of personal fulfillment in the process. I looked for a woman who, I thought, would make me happy and enrich the quality of my life. I married my wife, not as a heroic act of self-sacrifice exclusively for her benefit, but because I so enjoyed her company that I wanted to spend the rest of my life with her, and together we would experience the most intimate of human affinities. And my wife chose to marry me for substantially the same reasons.

We regard the love relationship as a reciprocal matter where mutual fulfillment takes place. Neither of us needs to suffer senseless guilt about "selfless love." My self is totally involved in my marriage even as my wife's self is totally involved in it. That totality of involvement is what makes the marriage relationship such a sensitive one.

No person on this planet has a greater ability to hurt me than my wife, because so much of my ego, indeed my soul, is invested in our relationship. She knows me more intimately than any other person does and, as a result, her acceptance or rejection of me counts most heavily.

No wonder divorce takes such a toll on the human psyche. How painful it is for anyone to reach the sad conclusion that the person who knows you best has rejected you. That realization casts a pall of fear over other relationships, as rejection looms as a constant danger. The masks go on and the walls go up, lest anyone else penetrates the naked soul and tramps on it.

Mutual Respect

An essential element in the traditional marriage ceremony is creeping toward the graveyard of anachronisms. The betrothal pledge includes a vow to "cherish" one's partner. To cherish means to assign a high value to something, to treasure it and to shield it from harm.

Selfish love does not cherish, but regards the spouse as a trivial object for self-gratification. The partner who is not cherished becomes a victim of exploitation. Mutual respect, not selfless love, is the antidote.

When I cherish my wife, I take pride in her and honor her. Smitten by the incurable disease of the romantic, I want my wife on the pedestal of Aphrodite; not on a platform of plastic glory, but the dais of love and esteem.

The practice of cherishing is a formidable defense against the casual affair which brings ruin to many marriages. Few affairs are initiated by calloused premeditation. Most of them take place "by accident," when crying needs which have suffered neglect inside the marriage are met outside the marriage.

Numerous times the facile explanation for the affair is offered, "She made me feel like a man again," or "He made me feel like a woman." The definition of what it means to feel like a man or to feel like a woman may be enigmatic, but the feelings are all too real.

The man who feels unesteemed by his wife is vulnerable to the admiration and respect he receives from his secretary. The woman who is taken for granted by her husband is vulnerable to the solicitous attention she receives from another male. Without malice aforethought, persons at such points of vulnerability can surrender almost involuntarily to the full-fledged affair.

A person can respond in different ways to the warm overtures of a third party. One can allow the ego to be titillated and encourage a deeper level of it, or one can view the overture as a clear and present danger to the marriage. The choice will be conditioned in part by the degree to which one cherishes and feels cherished in the marriage. But only a fool risks the loss of something priceless for a momentary massage of the ego.

How does cherishing move out of the abstract and into the concrete? How can I show my wife that I cherish her?

The answer echoes the reply of Elizabeth Barrett Browning: "How do I love thee? Let me count the ways."[1] One prominent marriage counselor said, "A woman needs to be told 365 days a year that she is loved and in 365 different ways."

The same applies to men. Though the macho image may preclude outward requests for assurances of love, the inward spirit craves them. Cherishing can be demonstrated in simple acts of appreciation and of sensitivity to the other person's needs.

Public Acknowledgment

A vital concrete display of esteem is the public declaration of love. I learned the importance of this from my own wife, who abides my outgoing displays of affection to countless female friends. I am the huggybear-type who hugs the ladies at the church door after the service and who fondly embraces feminine friends.

My wife assures me that she does not mind these outward displays of affection, leaving me a bit miffed by her equanimity. She

---

It is important for spouses to make their commitment to each other a matter of public knowledge.

---

explains that her security is established by the fact that I make it clear to the world that I am in love with her. She says she would lack that assurance if my proclamations of love for her were restricted to the privacy of our home.

It is important for spouses to make their commitment to each other a matter of public knowledge. That is why marriage services are not conducted in the backseats of cars at drive-in movies. When personal esteem is kept a secret, the marriage is open to invasion from outside.

Creative Intimacy

The sex life of the married couple is where personal esteem can either grow or languish. It is the inner sanctum of the union where the two become one flesh. A couple's sex life can be a scintillating spring or a fetid swamp where love is drowned.

God has made marriage a sacrosanct garden, the only estate in which sex is permitted. But within that garden, creativity must flourish if its fruit is to be abidingly fresh and delicious to the taste.

The Christian has suffered from the stranglehold of the ascetic who damns the delight of the Creator's gift. Where God is silent the Pharisees have howled, putting chains on the bedchamber where God has left us free. Taboos sully the garden and doom it to stagnation.

The ancient Manichaeans,[2] not the Hebrews, introduced the calumny that sex in marriage is at best a splendid vice or necessary evil. To the gallows with the Manichaeans who turn flowers into weeds and treasure into scrap. Let the marriage bed be undefiled as the apostle declared (see Heb. 13:4).

Defilement can spring from two directions: from the corruption of physical and emotional abuse or from the niggardly limits imposed by the prude. God's garden has walls, but those within are not confined to the space of a cell. The garden's landscape is vast, inviting exploration into its mysteries.

The sexual dimension of marriage is where couples meet; here in earnest quietude, there in breathless passion and over there in delectable frolic. Sex is at once serious and fun, reverent and playful, tender and exotic; as body meets body and soul joins soul.

Intimate Prayer
We can speak unabashedly of the enrichment of marital love that is sparked by the communion of prayer. But we must not see sex and prayer as polar opposites that drive a wedge into the harmony of personal communion. Prayer draws people close to each other as well as to God, inciting married people to deeper intimacy.

In paradise, the man and the woman stood naked and unashamed in the presence of God. The marriage bed affords us a taste of paradise regained.

CONFLICTS TO DIGNITY

Financial Conflicts
Marital disputes may be triggered by *conflicts of finance*. Such

strife is not limited to the poor; it afflicts affluent couples as well.

The problem is rooted in a basic series of facts. No one enjoys unlimited resources of wealth. Every couple faces the wall of the finite limit of money available for spending. At the same time, the desires for spending may approach the infinite.

The problem is compounded by the fact that no two people bring exactly the same value systems into the marriage. When the man wants new golf clubs and the woman wants a dishwasher, no problems arise if they have money enough for both. But if their funds are insufficient to cover both expenditures, something then has to give as the conflict point arrives.

Now is the point of sacrifice for one partner or both, as the value of the marriage must exceed the value of the checkbook. The marriage vow of "in plenty and in want" must come off the bench and into the game. The family budget must reflect a fair and equitable balance of the desires of both parties.

If a disproportionate sum of money is spent on the needs of one partner, the other partner feels devalued. The checkbook tells the story; it is a silent witness to disparity in the home.

Money is a medium of exchange, but also a medium of the measuring of value. Alone it can never determine the worth of love, but it does intrude into the realm of esteem. A wife is not a prostitute, nor a husband a gigolo whose esteem can be purchased with gold, but we need not prove it by penurious stinginess.

Mutual esteem conquers the clash of material values.

In-law Conflicts

In-law conflicts can be legion with interference raising its ugly head at multiple points. The father of the bride assumes territorial domain in his son-in-law's house. The mother of the groom criticizes the housekeeping of her daughter-in-law.

Manipulation and Interference. The quiet manipulation

game is played out where holiday meals are taken, and grand-parents countermand the discipline of the parents. Brother borrows and sister comes for overextended visits, expecting maid service from her hostess. Suddenly the newlyweds, committed to intimacy, become strangers in each other's world, locked out and isolated from each other by the interloping relatives.

Mother-in-law jokes are part of the American scene because they reflect a not-so-funny reality. Interference, however, is not the exclusive province of the much maligned mother-in-law, as any one of the in-law relationships can be troublesome. There are parents to whom no woman is worthy of their son, or no man worthy of their daughter.

The pain comes when offspring are caught in the excruciating vise of a loyalty squeeze. Being forced to choose between parent and spouse is an unholy coercion, leaving the dust of guilt to settle over the marriage. Competition replaces commitment, as affection is alienated by the race for favoritism.

Suppose, for example, the wife is the target of criticism from her husband's parents. She looks to her husband to be her shield and defender. For the husband the situation is double jeopardy.

If he defends his wife, he risks the alienation of his parents. If he sides with his parents, he demeans his wife. His position is not only precarious but painful, causing resentment to build within him against the pleas of his wife.

Leaving and Cleaving. For these reasons, part of the biblical institution of marriage calls the husband to *leave* his father and his mother and to *cleave* unto his wife (see Gen. 2:24). If the young couple is to have a chance for a successful marriage, the priority of value must be placed on their relationship, rather than on the gratification of the in-laws.

A real "leaving" and "cleaving" must take place. Here is an instance where the relationship of affinity takes preference over the relationship of consanguinity, making water thicker than blood.

Leaving of the parents is not equated with abandoning or rejecting them. The married children are still required to give honor to their parents; but the marriage estate must carry with it its own authority outside the sphere of parental authority. The parents are expected—indeed required of God—to respect the new family unit that the marriage has established.

Role Conflicts

The issue of *role conflicts* in marriage has been magnified in recent years with the rapidly-changing position of women in our society. Each partner brings to the marriage a certain prior understanding of what the role of the man and the woman should be. These role expectations are normally derived from observations in the home.

Conflict emerges when the role the wife expects to play in the marriage is not what the husband wants and vice versa. Imagine your partner's mother married to your father or your mother married to your partner's father. In one sense, that is what you have.

The dilemma of role-expectation rudely visited my marriage early. Since my wife and I dated for eight years before we wed, I was not expecting any surprises. But I got a whopper the first time I went on a business trip. As a matter of course, I asked my wife to pack my suitcase for me.

She looked at me in disbelief, saying, "What's the matter with you? Are you helpless? I'm not your slave. Pack your own suitcase."

I was deeply offended by her attitude and dutifully began to pout. I explained that my mother always packed my father's suitcase for him. She did not trust him to pack all he needed, so she assumed the task herself. My unspoken lament was, "If you loved me like my mother loved my father, you would be happy to pack my suitcase."

My wife explained that her father also went on frequent business trips and was fastidious about packing his own luggage. He did not want anybody touching his suitcase. My wife's unspoken thoughts were, "If he loved me like my father loved my mother, he wouldn't dream of asking me to pack his bags."

The whole business of packing suitcases was a domestic matter viewed from entirely different perspectives. To choose either route was to leave one party in the marriage feeling demeaned and unloved. The only solution to such problems is careful communication between husband and wife. The nature and source of role expectations must be sorted out in an atmosphere of respect.

DIGNITY AND DISCIPLINE

In the ancient world the bearing of children was viewed as a divine blessing. The more children, the greater the blessing. That cultural attitude has changed to one where the bearing of children is sometimes viewed as a curse, and the bearing of many children a bona fide calamity.

We have almost been brainwashed to believe that any more than two children is a disaster. The "unwanted child" has been the central justification for the legal abortions of over a million and a half unborn infants a year. Yet, in spite of the proliferation of abortions, the fact remains that thousands of child abuse cases are reported annually.

Extremes in Discipline
The battered child is not a valued child. One of the most important ingredients to valuing children is found in child discipline. Yet this very point of discipline is the most common point where parents go wrong. Discipline of children is a delicate art

which can be abused either in the direction of overseverity or in the direction of overindulgence.

The overindulged child is an unloved child. We hear the protests of parents to the contrary. When their offspring get in trouble, the parent wrings his hands in distress and asks mournfully, "Where did I go wrong? I gave the child everything he wanted."

One is tempted to answer the parent's cry by saying, "Do you really want to know where you went wrong? Let me give you a list." But such a rebuke at that point would merely add insult to injury.

Cycles in Discipline

The cultural syndrome tends to move in cycles. An indulgent generation is followed by a strict generation which, in turn, is followed by a new generation of indulgence. The cyclical pattern results from the children's resolve not to repeat the mistakes of their parents.

If a child grows up in a strict home and harbors resentment about it, he may resolve to be more lenient with his own children. On the other hand, a child who has been spoiled by overindulgence may realize that his undisciplined life is in part caused by the lack of discipline patterns established for him by his parents. He too may resolve to change that with his own children and overreact in the other direction.

In any case, self-discipline normally comes, not by magic, but as an extension of discipline imposed upon us by others.

Discipline as Training

The word *discipline* can be distasteful, having a harsh sound to it. Yet its meaning is integral to the Christian life, as discipleship is empty without it. Being a disciple under the tutelage of Jesus is a bit like being a raw recruit in the Marine Corps. Disciplined training with high goal expectations may be frightening, but it is affirming to human dignity.

Parents are not called to be marine drill instructors (D.I.s), but valuable lessons can be learned from the principles used in military training. The Marine Corps understands that to send an undisciplined recruit into battle is to send him to his death. The secret of discipline is to supply our children with the tools necessary to handle obstacles the future holds for them.

The slogan of the United States Marines, "The few, the proud, the marines," smacks of elitism. Yet that is precisely what the slogan is intended to communicate. The point they make is that it is not easy to become a marine. It requires intense work and discipline, but once one graduates he has self-esteem and confidence.

I witnessed a remarkable transformation of a classmate I knew from childhood. The boy consistently ranked at the bottom of the class, being a slow learner and slovenly in his personal habits. He was clumsy and awkward of foot, consistently chosen last when sporting teams were selected. He was rotund, and I do not recall ever seeing him at a school dance or hearing of any dates. He fit the expression "out of it."

High school graduation brought the inevitable breakup of the students who had been together throughout their school years. The majority of the graduates from our suburban community went on to college. I lost track of the obese young man, as he did not attend college.

My astonishment was without bounds when I encountered him while home on a college break. He appeared in the local drugstore, the favorite meeting place of our childhood group. I looked twice to be sure it was the same person, for the awkward, slovenly youth had been transformed into a walking recruitment poster for the marines.

He was smartly attired in Marine Corps dress blues with belt tightly drawn around a 28-inch waist. His posture was proudly erect, every hair was in place, and his swarthy features were now ruggedly handsome. The slogan, "The Marine Corps builds men," had come to life before my eyes.

I related this story to a friend who is a ranking general in the marines. I asked how it was possible to bring about such changes in young men. I spoke of the horror stories I had heard of Parris Island and of my recollections of Jack Webb playing the malevolent drill instructor in the Hollywood version of marine boot camp.

The general took the time to explain the process and philosophy behind the boot camp training of a marine. He said

---

The parent who neglects child discipline loves himself more than he loves the child.

---

the drill instructors have to be masters of playacting to convey the brutal image that strikes terror into the hearts of young recruits. And he revealed the necessity of having to change drill instructors frequently because it is hard on them to maintain the bad-guy image for a protracted length of time.

The drill instructors commonly met nightly, he added, to exchange ideas for improving their charade and to laugh together about the events of the day. The sadist has no place in the ranks of Marine Corps drill instructors.

The first stage of whipping recruits into shape is to motivate them by fear. They are driven through the first weeks of their training, treated like bits of raw sewage. Yet the point is not to destroy dignity but to build it.

After a few weeks of harsh training, at the moment when the average man nears the breaking point, the recruits are assembled in an auditorium to view a film. The film features the story of a young man who wants to become a marine. The sequence of his training unfolds on the screen as the lad is followed from the moment of induction to the head-shaving scene and step-by-step through his boot camp experience.

The actor is carefully chosen not to portray a sinewed athlete who could endure the training with ease, but one who mirrors the average recruit. The men watching the film hoop and holler as their comrade on the screen experiences all the things they have just endured. They cheer him on like Rocky against Apollo Creed when the recruit is confronted by an angry D.I. They identify with every small victory he achieves.

The screenplay follows the recruit through every stage the young marines have already passed through and then beyond to the final stage of camp—the magic moment when the young man on the screen is proclaimed a marine. The recruits cheer their film counterpart, rejoicing in his ultimate success. They leave the theater with the burning conviction that they too can make it.

This response on the part of the recruits is precisely what the film is carefully conceived to do—to convince the young men that they can make it if they will endure a few weeks longer. The feelings of hate toward their drill instructors slowly turn to love as it becomes apparent that these hard-boiled sergeants are really rooting for them to make it.

It must be underscored by repetition that parental discipline is not to be equated with the military specialty form of it. We need not shave our children's heads or roust them from their beds with a bugle call at 4:00 A.M. The principle is more basic—discipline can enhance self-esteem.

Discipline as Teaching
Discipline is a form of teaching, a setting of patterns which cannot be delegated to the exclusive responsibility of the school teacher. To withhold these tools is to rob the child of patterns

he both needs and craves. We spend hours coaxing our children to take their first hesitant steps, applauding their achievements as they stumble into our arms. But there is so much more to teach them, so many tools to equip them with that the infant patterns are but the beginning of disciplined training.

Discipline as Love

The wisdom literature of the Old Testament provides valuable insight as to the proper balance of discipline. The proverbial saying, "Spare the rod and spoil the child," is a corruption of the biblical text from which it is wrenched. The text reads, "He who spares the rod hates his son" (Prov. 13:24, *RSV*).

The idea of this proverb is at odds with much that passes for contemporary wisdom. In some circles, the spanking of children is regarded with such distaste that it is considered a type of cruel and unusual punishment. Lobby groups in some states have sought legislation making it a criminal offense for a parent to spank his child.

In these circles, spanking by parents is seen as manifestating a lack of love. Yet exactly the opposite conclusion is drawn from what the Bible teaches. For God's Word says failure to spank indicates a lack of love.

Why the discrepancy?

In biblical categories, spanking is valued as a means to the end of corrective discipline. The ultimate pattern for such discipline is found in the character of God Himself. We are exhorted not to despise the correction we receive at the hands of God, for "the Lord disciplines those he loves" (Prov. 3:12, *NIV*).

The parent who is indifferent to his child's development and who neglects the training of the child spares the rod, not out of a sense of charity, but because he seeks to avoid the unpleasant duty of administering discipline. Failure to discipline may indicate a lack of self-discipline on the part of the parent. The parent who neglects child discipline loves himself more than he loves the child.

Discipline as Respect

The difference between child-discipline and child abuse is vast. Parents are without excuse for abusing their authority by beating children or by subjecting them to public humiliation as part of corrective discipline.

The child must not be subjected to a reign of terror by a parent raging out of control. Nor must adolescents be subjected to infantile forms of punishment. The child's dignity is at stake and must be jealously guarded.

The New Testament enjoins us parents to "provoke not our children to wrath" (Eph. 6:4, *KJV*). This injunction sets the boundary of child discipline to what is fair and just. Severe forms of punishment and brutal attacks on the child, physical or verbal, are forbidden. Such abuse justly calls forth a reaction of anger from the child, for the child has not been treated with respect.

Discipline as Caring

Neglect, as well as severe punishment, can provoke the child to anger. If we fail to discipline, the message is conveyed that we really do not care. In a certain sense, the child wants to be disciplined and will, at times, push us to the edge of patience to make sure that we respond to him.

A little boy in a story by Freud illustrates how one child responded to being neglected. The little boy, expelled from school for being disruptive, then stood outside the classroom, pitching pebbles against the windows. When confronted for this added misdeed, the child explained that he just wanted to make sure the teacher knew he was still out there.

We know that children are not dogs and dogs are not children, but there are lessons to be learned from canine training methods. While I was administering obedience training to our dogs my daughter remarked to me, "Daddy, why is it that the dogs seem to like you more than they like me, even though you are the one who punishes them when they are bad?"

I responded, "Maybe that's why they like me. They know exactly what to expect from me and what their limits are. They also know what it is like to hear my praise for a job well-done."

I recall the first time I began obedience training with my two German shepherd puppies. The barrel-chested male resist-

---

To the aged belongs honor....They are the strength and continuity of the family, the patriarchal and matriarchal root of our own dignity.

---

ed the leash with such force that he snapped it in two. The female ran in fear and crept under the bed, refusing to come out. That was the first day.

By the third day, all I had to do was go to the closet where I kept the leash and rattle the chain, and the two dogs would fight each other, rushing toward me to see who could go through their training paces first.

I cannot remember competing with my sister to see who would get the first crack from my mother's wooden spoon. I took no delight in those administrations of discipline. But my memories of that spoon are almost fond, as I can laugh about the games we played, trying to hide it in perilous moments, only to discover that mother always seemed to have a suitable spare.

Our spankings were always followed by the warm hug and the careful assurance that we were still loved. Such actions did not generate confusion but merely confirmed the idea that we were being corrected precisely because we were loved.

Discipline Plus Time and Space

Children need more than discipline. The most valuable gift we can give them is our time.

They do not look to us to be their pals or their peers. They have their own lives to lead and rarely appreciate it if we refuse to allow them to be children or if we insist upon acting like them. The parent who tries too hard to be "one of the gang" is often an embarrassment to the child and is resented for his intrusion into their domain.

They need both space apart from us and access to us. We violate their persons if we seek to live our own lives again through them. They see through the game and gain no dignity from being used as alter egos.

The parent who values his child treats the child as one who is important in his own right.

DIGNITY AND THE AGED

The Cultural Stigma

It is fashionable today to speak of those in advanced years as "senior citizens." The change from "aged" or "elderly" to "senior" has come about, in part, as a response to our elders' protest against the stigma attached to growing old. We are told the world belongs to the young and aggressive, with the old considered worn-out and useless.

The respect for one's elders, found in ancient cultures and in many Eastern cultures today, has diminished rapidly in America. In the days before laws against age discrimination could be invoked as a protection, enforced retirement at age 65 carried the not-so-subtle message that persons beyond that age had little of worth to contribute to society. Even now, despite such laws and taking into account the supposed advantage of their accumulated experience, older job-seekers in our youth-oriented society still find that their maturity counts against them in interviews with younger personnel officers.

The Altered Perspective

As a teenager, I resented the patronizing advice of the elderly who looked down on me with a knowing smile that revealed a condescending tolerance to my zeal about matters. What frustrated me most was the refusal to give content-filled answers to my questions, opting instead for the infuriating dictum, "You will find out when you get older."

I countered the "experience is the best teacher" cliche with a proverb of my own, "Wisdom is in the head, not in the beard."

Time, however, has wreaked its vengeance upon me and, as my own hair becomes peppered with grey, I have a different perspective. I have lived through the awkward moments of answering my children's "why" questions with the feeble response of "because." I have faced the dilemma of finding no point of reference to explain those things I came to understand only through experience.

Certain things become more serious with age, while others lose their importance. The upset stomach is not assumed to be the flu by the older person, nor the headache merely a signal of fatigue. Every ache and pain must be considered as a possible sign of a life-threatening disease.

The outcome of sporting events is no longer a matter for tears. Changing moods are not measured in terms of days or hours but are measured in increments of decades.

The Total Anonymity

I returned to my alma mater to speak at a convocation exercise. As the event concluded, I walked from the cultural center along the walkway of the quadrangle toward the looming tower of "Old Main." There I saw a white-haired man shuffling along the walkway, teetering with his cane as students rushed by him with frightening speed, making his trek a dangerous one.

He was an octogenarian, almost 90. An out-of-style coat covered his stooped shoulders. I recognized him instantly as a former professor of the institution, a man who had attracted international acclaim in the decade of the '30s for his penetrating work in philosophy. He was once renowned for his scintillating intellect and insight.

I watched him now as he moved in total anonymity, with students brushing by him who were not worthy of carrying his briefcase. I thought to myself, *"The kids don't know this man, but God knows who he is."*

The Deserved Honor

When I see one bent with age, I see a person whose eyes have witnessed things I have only read about. The eyes are rightly called the "windows of the soul," revealing the pathos and suffering the soul has endured.

God calls us to honor and respect our elders in a special measure (see Lev. 19:32; Prov. 23:22; 1 Tim. 5:1). I find it difficult to pass a hoary head or see a wrinkled face without feeling a sense of admiration welling up inside me. The older person merits my respect, if for no other reason than that he has made it. He or she has survived.

The aged are the valiant ones who have gone too many times to the house of mourning, who have read too many obituaries in the paper, who have survived the rebellions of their children and the impertinence of their grandchildren. They know things we only guess about and exhibit a kindly patience toward our arrogance. They are hallowed people; sagacious, prudent and long-suffering.

Not all are saints, as some become irascible and others cantankerous. But the onslaught of senility or the embarrassment of incontinence cannot diminish the regal dignity of their person.

To the aged belongs honor. It is their sacred right to receive it, and our solemn duty to bestow it. They are the strength and continuity of the family, the patriarchal and matriarchal root of our own dignity.

FOR FURTHER REFLECTION

1. What makes you feel cherished?
2. What are the main reasons why people are enticed into extramarital affairs?
3. What are the principles which determine the limits of sexual practices between marriage partners?
4. How do in-laws interfere with married couples?
5. Discuss ways couples can clarify their role expectations.
6. Do you think spanking is a healthy form of discipline?
7. How does self-discipline or the lack of it affect your life?
8. What are the chief causes of teenage anger?
9. How do the elderly people you know feel about themselves?
10. How do people try to live their lives over through their children?

CHAPTER FIVE

DIGNITY IN THE SCHOOL

THE scene is Los Angeles, California. The building's architectural style reflects the modern flair of *nouveau* standards of West Coast culture, with sweeping walls soaring like the wings of birds toward the sky. At first glance, the style suggests a huge piece of contemporary sculpture, but the veteran eye perceives the lines of a fortress.

Inside the windowless walls, the tableau is chaotic. At the end of each hallway, a person stands whispering into a walkie-talkie as armed guards patrol strategic points of intersection. Students move at a frenetic pace between the monitors, scurrying between their classes.

It is a school, but the uninitiated mistake it for a prison. It is questionable who the captives are—the students or the teachers.

The school, especially the public high school, has become a combat zone. We have moved from the tranquility of the one-roomed school house on the prairie, presided over by the eastern school marm, to an armed camp complete with combat battalions and undercover narcotic agents. The modern scene makes Glenn Ford's *Blackboard Jungle* movie of the '50s resemble the proverbial Sunday School picnic.

Our schools have undergone a crisis of respect, touching the relationships between student and teacher, teacher and teacher, and teacher and administrator. The organization of teachers into a cohesive unit of collective bargaining is of recent vintage. In spite of better contracts, we are witnessing a mass exodus from the ranks of veteran teachers who are opting for early retirement. A common statement heard from them is, "Teaching is no longer fun."

THE DIGNITY OF THE TEACHER

The Attitudes of Society
America. The value of the teacher is placed at different levels in different societies. In America we tend to allow the value of the teacher to be dictated strictly by marketplace factors. The teacher seems doomed by the iron law of wages, as the profession has experienced a glut, with the surplus of teachers outnumbering the teaching positions available. The cliche is a byword, "Teachers are a dime a dozen."

But it takes more than a certificate to be a good teacher. The former cliche may be answered by another, "A good teacher is worth his weight in gold." From a monetary value system, the difference between a human being's weight in gold and a dime is astronomical. But we are a society that tends to measure the value of a professional by his salary level. From this perspective, it is hard to attach much worth to the teacher.

The value of a teacher also reflects the societal attitude toward education. Ours is pragmatically oriented, viewing education as a means to an economic end, placing a low level of value on the worth of education for its own sake or for the sake of character enrichment.

One of the great goals of my life was to be a college professor. The profession beckoned to me as a noble and exciting one. After 23 years of education, including 11 years of higher education, I was fortunate to secure an appointment to a college faculty in the northeastern United States.

I valued my position greatly, but was somewhat chagrined

We are a society that tends to measure the value of a professional by his salary level. From this perspective, it is hard to attach much worth to the teacher.

---

to read an article in the *Boston Globe* which revealed that the starting salary of the janitor in the Boston city schools was higher than mine—giving testimony to the law of supply and demand. This revelation did little to enhance my professional self-esteem.

Europe. All nations are not like America in placing the teacher on the lower rungs of the professional ladder. I experienced cultural shock when I began my graduate studies in a European university. I had enough orientation to know that I was expected to wear a coat and tie to my lectures, but I was still unprepared for my virgin exposure to the European system.

I entered the lecture hall and saw no sign of a professor. The students took their seats in orderly fashion with conversation muted. After a few minutes, the door opened and the professor entered. Instantly, the students rose to their feet and stood at attention until the professor reached the podium.

With a nod from him, the students took their seats and gave rapt attention to the lecture. The lecture was not to be interrupted by student questions, as it was considered presumptuous for a student to interrupt the professor's learned discourse which we were there to hear. But, to my everlasting horror, this lecture was interrupted not by a student, but by the professor himself.

It was a hot, stifling afternoon, without a zephyr in the air. To seek relief from the heat, I casually removed my sport coat. Suddenly the professor ceased his lecture in midsentence and glared in my direction.

He said icily, "Will the American student please put his coat back on?"

I was mortified as every critical eye was on me and, in my embarrassment, I wondered how the professor knew I was American. I quickly learned that the status of the student in the classroom was plebeian.

When the time came for my first oral exam I went through the necessary procedures to secure an appointment with the professor for the ordeal. I was surprised to discover that the exam would take place at the professor's home, a setting which made the occasion all the more intimidating.

From the moment I arrived, quaking in terror, I began to experience the metamorphosis of being changed from a plebe to a prince. Graciously ushered into the professor's study by his lovely wife, I was offered cookies and a choice among tea, coffee or Jenever—the shellaclike substance which the Dutch pretend is gin. An assortment of cigarettes and cigars was placed before me to use as pacifiers during the interrogation.

The demeanor of the professor was equally startling. He began the "exam" by inquiring earnestly into the satisfaction of my housing accommodations and the well-being of my wife and daughter. I hardly realized the moment when the conversation turned to academic matters.

Conversation is the accurate word as he proceeded to "test" me by holding a running conversation about the material I was studying, as if he were discussing the content with a peer. He made me feel like the most important person in the world and that my contribution to the discussion was valuable. At that moment, I understood that the classroom protocol was not an empty custom of traditional decorum.

Israel. The Bible is not silent about the role of the teacher. By divine mandate, we are called to give honor to our teachers. The role of the teacher in Israel was one of elevated status.

Jewish jokes abound about the pride of the Yiddish mother who speaks of "my son, the doctor" or "my son, the attorney." In Israel, the materfamilias spoke with the greatest pride when she could say, "My son, the rabbi."

So highly elevated was the status of the teacher that it had the power to reverse traditional matters of family etiquette. In the Jewish home, the father was treated with solemn outward signs of respect. His authority was acknowledged by visible signs of acquiescence.

The custom was for every child to stand when the father entered the room. That custom was broken on only one occasion. If the son was a rabbi, then it was the father who was required to stand when the son entered the room.

The New Testament underscores the awesome role of the teacher by declaring, "Let not many become teachers, for with teaching comes the greater judgment" (see Jas. 3:1). Christ warned of the dreadful consequences of judgment that would befall the teacher who was responsible for corrupting his student. He warned that it would be better for that person to have a millstone placed around his neck and be cast into the abyss than to cause one of the little ones to stumble (see Matt. 18:6).

The Role of Jesus

Christ Himself was a teacher, earning the right to the title "Rabbi." His was a peripatetic school in the literal sense, reflecting the style made famous by Aristotle's Lyceum. Jesus walked around as He taught, with His students following a few paces behind, committing their Master's teaching to memory.

The word *disciple* means "learner" or "pupil." When Jesus recruited His students, He used the standard rabbinic formula, "Follow me." We miss the force of that in our culture, interpreting it to mean the task of following a leader in other ways. Its meaning in the first century had a more literal connotation. The disciple was to follow his rabbi around on foot, walking behind him to hear his lectures.

The Bible reveals an intimate relationship between Jesus and His disciples, showing the degree of personal involvement the Rabbi had with His pupils. Christ required high standards of excellence from His disciples, and He engaged in a type of grading and promotion process.

The word *disciple* and the word *apostle* are frequently confused with each other and mistaken for synonyms. We do that because the New Testament speaks of 12 disciples and 12 apostles, and the groups are almost identical, save for the exclusion of Judas and the addition of his replacement, Matthias. We also see Paul, who was not one of the original 12 disciples, added to the ranks of the apostles.

The words *disciple* and *apostle* define two clearly distinguishable roles. An *apostle* is "one who is sent." He is a person commissioned to speak on behalf of and with the authority of the one who sends him. He functions somewhat like a modern ambassador or legate.

Not all of Jesus' disciples were promoted from the status of pupil or disciple to the rank of apostle. We know of at least 70 disciples who were enrolled in the school of Christ. Only 12 "graduated" to the rank of the apostle.

The respect shown to Jesus by His earthly pupils is the highest model we can find for the student-teacher relationship. It was the quintessence of honor and the acme of respect.

The Absence of Honor
A shameful and regrettable incident in my life took place when

I was in the ninth grade. Our class had been together as a unit through eight years of elementary school and had developed a fond relationship with our teachers; but ninth grade brought a new dimension. The school district, which included three other elementary schools from nearby towns, joined forces and constructed a new junior high school. We were excited to go there rather than face the gloomy prospect of being bussed to a

---

Christians seem particularly susceptible to the error that grace is a license for sloppiness or piety a substitute for performance.

---

depressed steel town and taking our junior high classes in an antiquated environment.

The first day was a bona fide disaster. We were greeted by a new homeroom teacher who presented herself as though she were a drill instructor for the WACS. In a stern voice, she laid down a rigid set of rules, giving notice that she intended to govern her domain with iron discipline.

Our initial fear turned to outrage as we responded to the challenge. A few of us got our heads together on the bus and vowed to bring the lady down. "She has got to go," was the consensus of the conspirators.

We laid out a plan of systematic harassment by classroom disruption, the throwing of cherry bombs in the aisle when her back was turned and outward acts of verbal insult and rude defiance— all of which earned us several trips to the principal's office. In less than a year she resigned, and we celebrated the "victory" over our vanquished enemy.

I did not see the woman or hear of her for 10 years until I met her one day in a supermarket. By this time, I was married and in graduate school. I was embarrassed to see her, as she appeared haggard and not nearly so formidable as she had through the eyes of a 14-year-old.

What followed was a long and disturbing conversation in which she revealed how painfully agonizing that year had been for her. She explained that the junior high was her first assignment as a teacher, having just graduated from college a few months earlier. She spoke of being apprehensive about facing a class of ninth graders and of adopting the facade of the stern disciplinarian to mask her own fright.

We never saw that fear, as we were too busy worrying about our own. When I saw the human side of this woman I felt sick at my stomach for the grief we had caused her. She tried to assuage my guilt by saying, "It's all right, I guess I was never really cut out to be a teacher."

Perhaps that explanation was true, but I knew within myself that we had never given her a fair opportunity to find out.

THE DIGNITY OF THE STUDENT

The Worth of the Student

Dignity in the school must include the worth of the student. The instruction of a human mind has life-transforming power. The shaping of the student's value system is greatly affected by the teacher, especially in what we call the "opinion-making" courses.

Every adult can mention at least one teacher who made a lasting impression on his life. It is easy to do after the fact, but most of us admit that our best teachers were the most demanding ones.

Even as children, we knew the difference between strictness and tyranny. We responded to the former and rebelled against the latter. Strictness and fairness are compatible, joined together in the good teacher, the teacher whose goal is to inform the minds of his students, not to rape them.

The Rewarding of Indolence

An indulgent teacher may be popular for a season, but harms the student by rewarding indolence. Christians seem particularly susceptible to the error that grace is a license for sloppiness or piety a substitute for performance.

I received an examination paper from a student in my theology class who wrote me a note at the bottom of his atrocious paper. He wrote: "Dear Professor Sproul, I'm sorry that I have done so poorly on this test, but I want you to know that I take Jesus as my Savior and have been blessed by your course."

I wrote below the student's remarks: "I am delighted that you have committed your life to Christ. In the Kingdom of God, you will be justified by your faith, but in this class, you will be graded for your works. You get an *A* for your faith, but an *F* for this exam."

Faith is to be shown in diligent action, not used as an excuse for sloth.

The Call to Excellence

The call to excellence that Christianity demands was impressed upon me when I was still on the other side of the teacher's desk as a seminary student, enrolled in an elective class of 22 students. I was surprised to discover that only one other student was taking the course for credit. The remaining 20 were present as auditors.

As I discussed this strange phenomenon with my classmates, I learned the reason for so many auditors was that they wanted to gain the benefit of the professor's marvelous lectures while avoiding the terror of his rigorous examinations. This professor was known to flunk second-semester seniors in courses required for graduation.

My classmates caucused and determined that something should be done about the exorbitant standards of the professor. I was elected to the unenviable task of being the spokesman to confront the professor about his grading system.

I knocked timidly on his office door and was cordially invited in for my "audience." I explained the dilemma of the students who both wanted his course material but feared his exams, and politely suggested he change his grading patterns.

He was kindly in his response, but submitted me to his favorite form of Socratic dialogue. The interrogation proceeded with a series of questions he posed.

"Do you think my examinations are unfair?"

"No, sir," I replied.

"Do you think that ministers are called to a high standard of excellence?"

"Yes, sir," was my response.

"Do you think the care of souls requires the best training possible?"

"Of course," I answered, as I experienced a growing sense of shame. I was the one who hastened the termination of the discussion, as his questions made me feel embarrassed for suggesting that the standards be compromised.

The Dynamic of Discipline

The same dynamic of discipline necessary in the home is carried over to the school. The teacher must walk that razor's edge between being overly indulgent and overly severe. Discipline must be upheld for education to take place.

The modern teacher is often hampered by a kind of double jeopardy. On the one hand, he must work with students who bring their lack of discipline to school with them. Some parents expect the teacher to perform a miracle of discipline by salvaging what the parent has abandoned.

On the other hand, the teacher faces legal restrictions imposed by the state or the local municipality. The teacher faces the current malaise in the schools and the Herculean task of wrestling with the problems while both hands are tied behind his back.

The Posture of Adversary
The teacher must avoid adopting an adversary attitude toward his students. When a combative mood exists the educational enterprise is in ruins. The atmosphere of learning is violated when the student is made to feel like an enemy.

I was distressed by my daughter's marked change in attitude as she made the transition from elementary school to high school. We were accustomed not only to excellent grade reports, but also to glowing compliments from her teachers about her pleasant disposition. That changed in high school, as a period of teenage apathy became evident, with the attending signals of dropping grades and the cessation of the glowing comments.

The change was not radical, as she did not become a juvenile delinquent. Neither was there a pattern of calls from irate teachers, nor evidence of adolescent drug abuse. But the change in her attitude was clearly observable, as she became apathetic about school rather than ebullient; indifferent to extracurricular activities rather than avid about them.

We were unable to elicit an explanation for the change, until after she was graduated and married. From the vantage point of the young adult, she reflected on that period of her life as a time of disappointment. Where once she loved school, she confessed that she came to hate it.

When I pressed for an explanation she replied, "I don't know exactly why, Dad, I just felt like in elementary school the teachers were for us, and at the high school they were against us."

No further elucidation was necessary, as it was evident her feelings on the subject were real. Whether they were justified or not is open to debate, but the fact persists that she felt as if the teachers were against the students. Of course, there were notable exceptions who went out of their way to show concern for the students.

The word *against* suggests an adversary posture where student and teacher are pitted in opposition to each other as antagonists. The adversary mood has deteriorated to the point of violence, with reports in the evening news of teachers being beaten, stabbed and shot to death by students. The street runs both ways, as incidents of child abuse and teacher brutality have likewise been reported.

Such incidents of violence cannot be tolerated either from the students or from the teachers. Expulsion is a viable option against violent and persistently disruptive students, as education is not an inalienable right for the destructive student.

The Policy of Tenure

If student morale is to be elevated, then we must view the policy of teacher tenure with the philosophy of the second glance. No violent, incompetent or indifferent teacher should be allowed to hide behind the fortress of tenure. Tenure is a practice which does little to add quality to education and much to destroy it.

The presence of a surplus of qualified teachers should work in favor of increased excellence in the field. Where competition is stifled by tenure, the school becomes a closed shop, and the performance level of the entrenched incumbents takes a downward spiral. It affords the incompetent teacher a level of job security unheard of in most segments of the professional world.

If the student is valued and his education a priority, then we must begin to evaluate teachers on the basis of their principal task, which is teaching. We are aware of the multitudes of teachers who have impressive educational credentials but poor teaching skills. They are hired for their impressive academic credentials, which add prestige to the institution that hires them. But such prestige is gained at the expense of the students who must endure their inept attempts at pedagogy.

The Ability to Communicate

Teaching is an art that requires more than knowledge. It requires the ability to communicate that knowledge to the student. The ignorant teacher who is a skilled communicator entertains the student without educating him.

If we must choose between the two, we are left with the devil's choice. And we should not have to choose between these grim alternatives. If we reward the teacher who knows his subject and knows how to teach it, we can overcome the malaise engendered by the present system.

FACULTY LOYALTY

Teacher-Teacher Relationships

Teacher-teacher relationships are also important. The interpersonal attitudes of the teachers spill over into the classroom. If one teacher uses his podium as a soapbox to castigate the views of other teachers, the student suffers. Though the game is often played subtly, the students recognize it and are frequently offended by the pettiness of it.

At times, students will encourage internecine warfare among the faculty and egg them on in the classroom. A lasting impression about interfaculty loyalty was made on me by my seventh-grade history teacher who doubled as our basketball coach. He was beloved of the students, especially by the athletes who were somehow permitted to address him by the abbreviated form of his last name, "Mac"—at least outside the classroom. In class, he was "Mr. MacIntyre."

One thing sparked his temper, bringing fire to his eyes and the look of steel to his angular jaw, and was met with frigid rebuffs whenever it was attempted by his students. That was talking about other teachers behind their backs.

If a student raised his hand and said, "Mr. MacIntyre, this

morning in science class, Mr. Gregg said...," that is as far as the student would get.

Mac would cut him off in midsentence with the same response every time, "I'm not interested."

Sometimes the student would protest and try to continue, "But, Mr. MacIntyre, I only...."

And again, the words would come down like a hammer, "I'm not interested."

That said something to us about loyalty. As much as we prized having Mac on our side, we could only respect him for refusing to be used as a foil against one of his teaching colleagues.

Teachers and Others
Someone shortchanged by the gods of wit said recently, "America is having so many strikes, she is beginning to look more like a bowling alley than a republic." We are inured to the strike that shuts down the coal mine or the loading dock, but we recoil when our schools are closed and the teachers "hit the bricks."

The sight of teachers parading in picket lines pricks the bubble of idealism which is traditionally linked to the profession. The tradition totters as precariously as the fiddler on the steeply pitched roof. And, as community resentment rises against the teachers, parents take offense that their children are "cheated" of precious learning time.

The teachers march to show their feelings of being "cheated" by the guardians of the public purse strings. They have organized to make their cry heard, as they are embittered by being taken for granted and considered of little value. The school board meeting place has become a new arena of labor-management strife, and our children are caught in the middle. The protracted teacher strike has been a disruptive force in the local community, threatening the hopes of parent-teacher solidarity. At issue are not merely economic concerns, but issues of dignity.

Both the teacher and the student have an aching void. That void must be filled, if we are to change the school from a combat zone to a place of learning. We are playing a most serious game here, where the stakes are nothing less than the minds of our children.

When we ignore the teacher we punish his pupil. When we respect the teacher we honor his student.

FOR FURTHER REFLECTION

1. Do you favor compulsory education?
2. How are teachers evaluated in your school system? What are their pay scales?
3. What do you think of the European system of formal decorum?
4. What do you think of grading students?
5. What makes students feel their teachers are against them?
6. How are the schools in your neighborhood handling drug problems?
7. List the most important qualifications for a teacher.
8. How are the school teachers of your area related to the total life of the community?
9. Should teachers' life-styles be considered in their hiring and firing? Explain.
10. How has your community handled teacher strikes?

CHAPTER SIX

DIGNITY IN THE HOSPITAL

WHEN Wayne Alderson conducted his first Value of the Person seminar in a hospital, the concern of administrators, nurses and physicians quickly converged on the central motif of the value of the patient. The hospital primarily exists not as a marketplace for the doctor or as a laboratory for research, but as a place of healing for those afflicted by disease or injury. Though the Hippocratic oath[1] is now a matter of history, it embodied in its creed the central importance of the well-being of the patient.

In recent years, increased attention has been paid to the emotional and psychological needs of the patient, as the medical profession realizes the truism that it is as important to prepare the patient for surgery as it is to prepare the surgery for the patient. The advent of holistic medicine has underscored this factor.

We easily overlook the remarkable advances medicine has made in the last century and a half. The practice of antiseptic procedures to avoid the transfer of deadly bacteria from one patient to another was unknown to our great-grandparents.

The childbirth mortality rate of both infants and mothers was inordinately high just a little over a century ago, when it was standard practice for a physician, after having done a post-mortem on a corpse, to move directly into the delivery room and preside in a childbirth procedure without taking the time to wash his ungloved hands.

Soldiers wounded on the battlefields of the Civil War faced the removal of bullets and the amputation of limbs without the

---

Fear of pain and fear of death are two of the most potent forces in our lives.

---

benefit of sophisticated pain-killing drugs. The miracle drugs called antibiotics which have disarmed the potency of several virulent diseases, and the new vaccines which have removed the threat of many dreaded illnesses, have appeared only in the last 50 years.

It is almost impossible to keep pace with the geometric progression of the advance of modern medicine. New transplant procedures, bypass heart operations and the use of computerized diagnostic methods have added significantly to man's life expectancy. Today's patient enjoys enormous benefits of medical care that his ancestors never dreamed possible.

Yet with all these advances, there is still room for improvement, particularly in maintaining the dignity of the patient. The benefits of mechanized medicine have come with a price tag. The days of doctors' house-calling are over; the surgeon's personal bedside attentions are usually limited to abrupt one- or two-minute visits, as the emotional care of the patient has been delegated to nurses, therapists, aides and orderlies, and sometimes even to the cleaning lady.

DIGNITY IN FEAR AND HUMILIATION

Two nagging problems remain to be solved in hospital relations with patients. The twin menaces of the patient are *fear* and *humiliation.*

The Fear Factor

To speak in universal generalizations is dangerous, but we can make one universal affirmative without question of contradiction: *every patient who enters a hospital experiences some level of fear.*

No matter the patient's outer mask of bravado, those attending the patient can assume that anxiety is present. And the fear factor can be serious enough to inhibit the healing process and to cause unexpected trauma during and after surgery.

Fear of pain and fear of death are two of the most potent forces in our lives. This fear element is what makes us define major surgery as any surgery performed on us; minor surgery only happens to other people.

The Humiliation Factor

The humiliation factor is also critical. The patient confined to a hospital room often feels helpless and vulnerable.

The clothes he wears to enhance his self-esteem are removed in favor of the backless hospital gown; his pin-stripe suit or favorite sweatshirt tucked away in the closet. Women are denied their attractive outfits and hairstyles, as the beauty parlor is not accessible to the in-patient.

The Lack of Privacy. The elderly are required to yield their dentures to the nightstand, thereby losing their dignity and privacy in the fishbowl exposure of the ward. Even in the semiprivate room, intimate examinations are performed and bodily functions are carried out behind the hopelessly inadequate screen of a lightweight curtain.

Finally, add the ignominy of the bedpan—the last of ancient

hospital instruments to be improved upon—and the last shred of human dignity disappears.

The Element of Embarrassment. Unfortunately, no foreseeable way exists to eliminate the humiliating and embarrassing elements of hospital care entirely. To be dignified when you are sick is just plain hard.

I spoke with one venerable woman who in her normal state of health is the epitome of dignity. During a round of chemotherapy treatments for a malignancy, she suffered the side effects of nausea. She accepted the discomfort stoically and said it was a small price to pay for the therapeutic value of the medication. She added, however, the observation that "it is difficult to be dignified with your head in the toilet."

I faced embarrassing moments when I went into the hospital for surgery as a young man. I was suffering from hemorrhoids which had refused to surrender to the supposedly magical power of Preparation H. Mine was not a life-threatening malady, but I suffered from anxiety attacks anyway.

The worst part of the experience was not the pain of recovery, which was minimized by the great relief of knowing the surgery was behind me (no pun intended), but the procedure I endured the day before surgery. In addition to the manual rectum examination by the presiding surgeon, I endured the sometimes clumsy probing of no less than five additional persons. These were examinations undertaken by interns who were using me as their pedagogical "Exhibit A."

I kept telling myself that this exercise was all for the cause of advancing their education and that some poor soul would one day benefit from my present discomfort. Yet I did reach a point where I felt like a piece of meat hanging in a butcher shop for everyone's inspection.

My growing anger was exceeded only by my fear that Intern Number Six would soon walk through the door and put me through this humiliating show-and-tell routine once again. I am not an expert in medical training, but I cannot help thinking that there must be a better way.

The Compassion Factor

The indignity I experienced at the hands of the interns was (no, I cannot use the word "rectified") remedied the next day as I began postoperative care. When I awakened from the anesthesia and was taken back to my room, the attending nurse explained the intervals set for my pain-killing drugs and instructed me on the use of the call button to summon her when I

The nurse has many roles to perform....
The more difficult...is that of
mediator...between doctor and patient.

---

needed help. The shots were to be given every four hours as the effect of the drug wore off and the pain intensified.

After my first four hours, no one magically appeared to administer another dose. I was reluctant to use the call bell for fear of being considered a sissy. I endured the pain as long as I could, which was about another 30 seconds, until I humbled myself and pressed the button.

Instantly, the nurse appeared with another injection ready. I greeted her with profuse apologies, saying, "I'm sorry to bother you. I know there are lots of people in here who are in far worse shape than I am."

She smiled kindly and replied, "There may be people here who are more seriously ill than you are, but there is no one in this hospital who is experiencing more pain."

I did not believe her for a second, but her words restored my honor for she made me feel like a hero.

Nurses have a way of administering compassion that touches the soul as well as the body. My second trip to the hospital was for an operation on the cartilage of my knee. I developed some postoperative complications which had me sweating in agony.

A matronly nurse came to my room at midnight and sat with me for hours, wiping my brow and holding my hand. Her medicine was as important to me as the antibiotics that were flowing through my bloodstream. That woman valued me and preserved my dignity in a trying moment.

THE DIGNITY OF THE NURSE

It is not only the patient who must be esteemed in a hospital situation. The staff personnel are also subjected to indignities and disrespect. The difficult patient vents his pain and frustration on whoever comes his way.

The Indignities

The nurse is a skilled professional whose ministrations are vital to the well-being of the patient. Yet nurses are often mistreated by cantankerous patients who, like mean drunks, are transformed into savages by the onslaught of illness. I have witnessed a patient throwing her breakfast tray in the face of a nurse and unleashing tirades of obscenities against housekeeping personnel.

The Disrespect

Because the nurse acts in a serving role, she—or he, as the case may be—is often regarded as a servant. The very presence of the call bell leads some patients to act as though they have a butler or maid at their beck and call. Such patients adopt an imperious attitude toward the nurse as if the nurse had no other calling in life than to cater to the whims of the individual patient.

The Battle

The nurse has many roles to perform. She must be a teacher, a secretary, a "mother," a medical technician and a "priest." One of the more difficult roles she assumes is that of mediator. She stands between the doctor and the patient. If she is treated brusquely by the physician and rudely by the patient, she must battle for her dignity on two fronts.

THE DIGNITY OF THE DOCTOR

The Professional Status

In recent decades, especially since the emergence of the medical specialist, the status of the doctor has climbed to the very heights of the professional ladder. The higher fees that go with specialization have impelled a steady rise in physician affluence. With the increase in wealth and prestige have also come a growing resentment and envy from the general public.

The Public Image

As the doctor becomes more inaccessible, he garners the image of the aloof high priest or the elite Olympian who only cares about multiplying his wealth. The image of the folksy frontier doctor who scurries about with his little black bag, delivering children, treating the measles and taking time out to offer advice about family problems, is gone.

The modern image of the doctor is frequently that of a wealthy playboy who is more interested in the latest stock market report than the medical journal. He is cast in the role of the cocktail party fixture who seduces every nurse in sight. On TV, Marcus Welby has been replaced, first by Trapper John and now by other swinger-doctor types. The image is not complete without the vision of the doctor spending most of his time at the country club playing golf.

The Hard Reality

There are wealthy doctors and, undoubtedly, some are philanderers, but the image is a caricature. I love to play golf, but I hate to play it with doctors. One of the great attractions about the game of golf is the absence of telephones on the golf course—except when you are playing with physicians.

Who enjoys carefully lining up a six-foot putt, only to have your concentration rudely disturbed by the sound of the doctor's beeper? Who enjoys playing seven holes of golf only to look up and see the assistant pro coming in a golf cart to take your playing partner away because of an emergency call? Rarely have I been able to complete a full 18 holes of golf with a physician.

Doctors are always on call, a beeper tone away from urgency. Their lives are not nearly as glamorous as they appear. Walk with them through one week of their lives and see if you begrudge the money they make.

Their wealth is often over-estimated, and few people are aware of the overhead costs of their profession. The cost of malpractice insurance is now so high that doctors pay more for their malpractice premiums than most people make in a year. The doctor has become the prime target of the professional ambulance-chaser.

The Closed Shop

The physician's life is stress-filled, making him one of the highest-ranked professionals on the list of potential suicide and burnout victims. And ironically, part of the explanation for the harried life of the doctor is found in the fact that there are too few doctors for too many people. For nowhere is a surplus of physicians meeting the needs of the community.

Why?

Because the medical profession is rapidly becoming a closed shop at the expense of the public. The practice of medicine is still a noble profession and worthy of honor. Not everything about the profession, however, is bathed in altruism.

Restricts the Competition. Admittedly, with the law of supply and demand and with the income level of the physician, one would think that young, competent students would be flocking to medical schools to train for the profession. As a matter of fact, multitudes of such students—coming from the highest levels of college graduates—are applicants for admission. Yet the specter of the campus valedictorian being denied entrance to medical school is not a rare one.

How nice to think that the reason for such high admission standards is found in the concern to protect the public from damage wreaked by incompetent physicians. Such a conclusion, however, would be naive, for the accrediting agencies have more in view than standards of medical excellence. What is also operating is the desire of already licensed physicians to keep their ranks small and free from too much competition.

Lessens the Excellence. By keeping their numbers small, they insure that the market value of their time and services is kept at a premium. Nothing lowers prices like competition. The tragic irony of this pattern is that the closed shop foisted on the public in the name of concern for high standards of excellence restricts competition, which is one of the strongest forces for excellence.

Inconveniences the Public. The scarcity of physicians also subjects the public to another annoying phenomenon—the interminable wait in the doctor's waiting room. A certain percentage of this inconvenience cannot be avoided, as the physician's time schedule is difficult to predict with accuracy. His office hours are interrupted by emergencies, and the maladies presented to him differ from case to case in terms of the time required to treat them.

Yet we all know what it is like to have a scheduled appointment with the doctor, only to be kept waiting for two or three hours before we get in to see him. The message that comes through to the patient is that the patient's time is not valuable. Those of us in other professional positions involving scheduled appointments know the ire of people who are provoked when they are kept waiting.

The People Concern

Medical care is a people concern. The doctor, the nurse, the hospital staff, indeed all who labor for the relief of human suffering are on the front lines of the battle for human dignity. And where the ill are valued, the whole of human dignity is elevated.

FOR FURTHER REFLECTION

1. Why has the Hippocratic oath been discarded?
2. What things can be done to minimize patient fear?
3. Should patients be required to grant permission for student probing of their problems? Why? Why not?
4. How can nurses be protected from unruly patients?
5. Do you favor greater government involvement in medicine? Why? Why not?
6. Do you favor the increase of medical schools to supply more medical professionals? Why? Why not?
7. List the diseases that have been eliminated or greatly reduced in threat and severity in your lifetime.
8. Do you favor more government subsidies for medical research? Why? Why not?
9. What is the image of the doctor in your community?
10. How could medicine become more personalized?

CHAPTER SEVEN

DIGNITY IN THE PRISONS

TO speak of the value of the person in a prison sounds like an anomaly. The prison inmate is one of the least valued persons in our society. Terms like *love, dignity* and *respect* are not included in the daily nomenclature of the penitentiary.

Prisoners as Economic Burdens

The "value" of the prisoner may be measured in economic terms as it costs the taxpayer in excess of $20,000 per year per inmate to keep a person incarcerated in a correctional institution. For this reason, among others, the prison inmate is seen more as a burden than as a valuable commodity to society.

Few people have ever visited the inner chambers of a maximum security prison. We have images provided by Hollywood and television, but the impact of real life escapes us. It is normal for human beings to isolate criminals from society and equally normal for us to isolate ourselves from the criminal's situation once he is behind bars.

Prisoners as Human Beings

The prisoners' plight as captives is one in which we have little interest, as we prefer the insulation of ignorance. We have enough problems facing the pain and misfortune of noncriminals who clamor for our compassion without being bothered by those who have committed heinous acts of crime against society. Yet, criminals are still people and their claim to human dignity is not vitiated by their crimes.

Charles Colson, former Nixon White House aide, convicted and imprisoned for his role in the Daniel Ellsberg/Pentagon Papers episode, got me interested in the contemporary criminal justice system. Colson, author of *Born Again* and *Life Sentence*, heads the national organization known as Prison Fellowship, devoted to making Christian principles operative in prisons everywhere. His book, *Life Sentence,* is an absorbing documentary on life in America's penal institutions.

THE DENIGRATION OF DIGNITY

Colson escorted me on my first visit to a maximum security prison. The impressions of that sojourn were indelibly imprinted on my mind as I experienced the somber reality of the "inside." Driving up to the visitors' entrance of the large midwestern state penitentiary, I had the feeling of approaching a docile college campus.

Seeing the Outside Image
The outer grounds were immaculate, displaying verdant acres of carefully manicured landscape. No outward sign of barbed wire or gun turrets betrayed the real purpose of the edifice. The atmosphere was serene, again conjuring up the image of the peaceful environs of an educational academy.

Experiencing the Inside Reality
Cold Austerity. As I entered the building and moved to the visitors' quarters, I noticed a change of ambience. That I was not

in the registrar's office of a university was immediately apparent. The atmosphere was chilled by the cold austerity of the place.

Strident Language. Hard wooden benches and concrete floors were spaced within the drably painted walls whose monotonous blankness was broken by posters announcing harsh warnings to visitors. Words like "please" or "are requested" were noticeably absent from the copy of the posters. The strident language used in the posted instructions made this visitor feel as if he were an inmate himself.

One corner of this area was adorned by the artwork of inmates. The gallery selections appeared to have been made by someone with a cruel sense of art depreciation, as the samples displayed were of a garish sort, ranging from the primitive to the hideously grotesque. The scenes depicted in some of the paintings were of sordid violence bordering on the surreal. I wondered how a relative of an inmate would feel in this depressing atmosphere.

Steel-barred Doors. From the visitor section, we were escorted to the inner chamber containing the prison complex itself. We had to pass through a double strata of electronically controlled steel-barred doors to go through security. As we left the second area, we heard the sound of the steel doors being clanged shut. The hearing of that sound reminded me of the origin of the slang designation for the prison as the "slammer."

Hardened Men. My next impression was of the faces of the inmates themselves. We received furtive glances from some who did their best to appear tough and hostile. The looks we got did their job, as feelings of fright were awakened within us and all notions of being on a mission of mercy to poor unfortunates were dispelled. We were in the company of hard men, some of them ruthless in their capacity for brutality. I was glad that another set of bars separated me from some of the more violent-looking types.

Shabby Surroundings. The auditorium was equally depressing. The floors were of concrete and the uncomfortable chairs were in need of paint. The shabby stage reminded me of my surreptitious visit to The Casino, Pittsburgh's famous landmark of vaudeville and burlesque, where I went as a teenager to view the performance of Georgia Southern.

The curtains on the prison stage were threadbare and torn in places. The broken ivory keys of the antiquated piano had long since turned to yellow. Trying to get the microphone system to work was an exercise in futility, as the only sound it would emit was that of a 60-cycle hum.

Limited Budgets. I asked the chaplain how he was able to put on religious services with such antiquated equipment. He revealed that his annual program budget to provide for the spiritual needs of his 2,000-member congregation was set at $5,000. I wondered what would happen to a church of 2,000 members that tried to operate with a similar budget.

Monotonous Routine. The speakers for the day were Colson and Lem Barney, the distinguished veteran all-pro cornerback for the Detroit Lions. The celebrity status of the speakers helped draw about 300 inmates to this voluntary event. Added to the drawing appeal was the break from the monotony of daily routine.

Hostile Audience. At the outset the attitude of the audience was hostile. A group of mean-looking men who were obviously high on drugs sat next to me. As Colson began to speak, he was greeted with catcalls and other verbal insults, and I had the growing feeling that our presence there was unwise.

Presenting the Suffering Savior

A Relevant Message. The guards were growing uneasy as well, until Colson moved more deeply into his address. He spoke of the ordeal of Christ in the prison of Jerusalem, of His treatment at the Praetorium and of His trial before Pilate. The catcalls ceased as the audience warmed to the speaker.

An Anointed Speaker. I have heard Charles Colson speak many times on the outside at prayer breakfasts, church conferences and other types of assemblies. He is a polished communicator with an effective and engaging style. But when he spoke in the darkness of that prison, a different aura came over him which gives definition to the concept of "anointed" speaking.

An Empathetic Presentation. His identification with the misery of his audience came across strongly, as compassion exuded from his being. Even the most calloused of that inmate audience was moved by Colson's message. Somehow, he elicited a spark of hope in them and restored, if but for a few moments, a sense of dignity.

Enjoying the Gospel's Impact

Spontaneous Appreciation. At the conclusion of the meeting, a spontaneous outburst of warmth and appreciation was bestowed upon all of us who took the time to reach out to these men. The guards were frightened, but helpless to stop the surge of the prisoners as they rushed to thank us and to throw their arms around Colson and Barney in grateful embrace.

A guard used the loudspeakers to give direction for our orderly exit from the auditorium. First, the prisoners were removed and then we were herded together, flanked by armed guards, to exit as a unit. As we passed the cell block, separated from the corridor by bars filled with glass windows reinforced by wire caging, a crowd of prisoners pressed up against the doors, waving and shouting greetings to us.

Genuine Fellowship. Several window panels were missing, and the inmates stretched out their arms in an effort to touch us and shake our hands. Colson broke ranks and started to move in the direction of the cell block. Two guards moved to block his path, as he turned to me and said, "Let's go, R.C."

As we moved together toward them, a rousing cheer went up from the inmates, and the guards moved aside to let us through. We grasped the hands that were extended through the bars and looked into the faces of the teary-eyed men. The angry scowls were gone as their hardened faces melted with appreciation.

Chuck looked at me and said, "The excitement of the Republican National Convention could never match this."

Profound Satisfaction. As I left the confines of the prison, I carried with me a profound sense of satisfaction, for at least on one occasion I fulfilled a direct mandate of Christ to visit those who are in prison (see Matt. 25:36; also Heb. 13:3; 1 Pet. 3:19). Since that initial visit, I have had many other experiences in prisons and considerable exposure to inmates, as we regularly hold seminars for them.

Understanding the Prison System

Undefined Purposes. The prison system is made complex by the fact that the prisons serve no single clearly-defined purpose. Prisons are considered useful for a plurality of reasons and have been modeled to carry out a wide variety of purposes, some of which are in contradiction to each other. The name *penitentiary* comes from the Quaker origin of the term designed to describe a place where penance could be exacted from criminals.

Some view the prison as a place where retributive punishment is administered for the sake of justice. Others place the accent on the protection of the public from those who represent a threat to safety. Still others view the role of the prison as being chiefly that of an institution for rehabilitation.

Differing Conditions. Different levels of prisons range from release-time detention centers or halfway houses to the maximum security facility. Conditions vary from prison to prison and from state to state, as well as from state to federal to municipal structures. Antiquated facilities, accelerating costs and the problem of overcrowding, all add to the difficulty of maintaining a humane criminal justice system.

Growing Numbers. At year end 1989, the number of inmates in America's state and federal prisons was a record 710,054 men and women. This figure represents an increase of 115 percent in the prison population from 1980 to 1989. The increase in inmate numbers was 12.5 percent from 1988 to 1989 alone. "The 1989 increase meant a nationwide need for more than 1,600 new prison bedspaces per week."[1]

Competing Solutions. This accelerating "boom" in greater numbers of new prisoners being added to the prison population every year prompts competing cries for government action to resolve the crisis. One faction argues for more and larger prisons, "so we can get all those crooks off the street, lock them up and throw away the key." Others, recognizing the horrendous costs of keeping enormous populations behind bars, argue for early release programs to ease the burden on the taxpayer who must at some point foot the bill.

HIDDEN INDIGNITIES

The establishing of an equitable system of criminal justice is no easy matter. Even the issue of fair standards of sentencing is made cloudy by the imposition of mitigating circumstance to the judge's decision and by the complexities arising out of plea bargaining.

Disparate Sentences

The disparities of sentences that exist among those convicted of similar crimes is patently obvious to anyone bothering to examine the situation. In addition to these inequities is the serious problem of hidden punishments attached to the prisoner that are not a formal part of the penalty imposed by the courts.

Homosexual Rape

The clearest example of the hidden penalty is the matter of homosexual rape. The incidence of this kind of assault rises proportionately with the level of institution to which a convicted felon is assigned.

At the worst level, the rate reaches an astonishing 99 percent. That is, if a person 30 years or younger is sent to a maximum security prison, the probability factor is 99 percent that he will

---

Guarding an offender's humanity is not coddling the lawbreaker.

---

be subjected to homosexual rape within the first 48 hours of his incarceration. That is the harsh reality of prison life.

Charles Colson was once guided to a secluded area of a maximum security prison and shown where this atrocity was customarily performed beyond the purview of the guards. The stones on the floor were permanently stained red from the blood that flowed from the rectums of the victims.

The percentages given are not a result of hyperbole, but an accurate assessment of the real situation. Rape is not an isolated problem, but is at such epidemic proportions that assignment to a maximum security prison almost guarantees it. The occurrence of rape is so commonplace as to be an accepted part of the penalty imposed for the crime.

The physical pain and possible damage of homosexual rape have been well documented, but who can measure the damage to human dignity that it imposes? The humiliation that attends such an ordeal can scar the soul forever.

Yet homosexual rape is not the only form of indignity suffered by prison inmates. The entire prison experience, in many cases, exposes a person to the systematic destruction of human dignity. If prisoners are not "animals" at the time of their incarceration, they almost inevitably will become so. The destruction of self-respect is a major contributing factor to the alarming rate of recidivism that plagues our criminal justice system.

Strip Searches
The process of destroying the dignity of the prison inmate begins the moment he arrives at the penal institution. After he is escorted through the slamming steel doors and duly registered, he is routinely subjected to a strip search to insure against the possibility of smuggling contraband into the prison. In a posture of nakedness, he is checked thoroughly, with every bodily orifice carefully examined.

The effect of being reduced to nudity has a profound psychological impact on the new inmate. Though the necessity of this practice may be defended in terms of the need to stem the tide of controlled substances and other contraband, it can be carried out in ways which are less offensive. Ancient warriors understood the psychologically destructive impact on an individual of nudity compelled, a power which they exercised by forcing their conquered enemies to march publicly, chained and stripped, in the humiliating state of nakedness.

Even in the formal circumstances of a medical examination, being unclothed while under the gaze and inspection of another is difficult. The prison inspection routine, to be humane, must apply the sensitive safeguards of the physician, so the inmate will not be intentionally humiliated by the strip search.

Some prison administrators, however, defend a more rude form of the procedure, deliberately undertaken to "break the spirit" of the new inmate, lest he quickly become a troublemaker. When this procedure occurs, the assault against dignity is made an integral part of the criminal's punishment.

Yet guarding an offender's humanity is not coddling the law-breaker. Taking such precautions only serves to underscore the importance of human dignity and ultimately benefits all who are human.

Used Underpants

From the strip search, the convict is moved to the department where he is issued his prison clothing. Imagine the feeling of the man when he is handed a pair of undershorts that have already been used by four or five previous prisoners.

The "used underpants gambit" is not employed as a measure to trim budgets or to economize. The savings achieved by such a measure are irrelevant. Here we have a clear example of psychological warfare that is intentional.

The game involves a purposed insult to the incoming prisoner to "put him in his place." No penal institution which includes rehabilitation as one of its goals could ever tolerate this kind of abuse of the prisoner's psyche. The person who is systematically subjected to overt or subtle assaults on his self-worth has little hope of ever being rehabilitated.

RESPONSES TO INDIGNITY

The nation has been rocked by a series of violent uprisings in maximum security prisons from Attica, NY (1971) to Santa Fe, NM (1980) to Moundsville, WV (1986). In these and other similar incidents, unbridled violence has erupted with hostages taken and killed and fellow inmates slaughtered. Add to this carnage the self-destructive acts that occur when the inmates go on a rampage and destroy their own facilities—as they did at the Lorton, VA prison complex near Washington, DC (1986)—evidencing the self-defeating action of cutting off one's nose to spite his own face.

What makes people behave like that?

The Criminal's Response

The psyche of the criminal is as complex as a road map of New York City. The psychiatrist may be able to penetrate Manhattan and the Bronx, but he does not reach Brooklyn. It would be foolish to guess the plethora of reasons that would totally explain these behavioral patterns.

Retaliation. One factor, however, must be included in the list. When people are subjected to a systematic destruction of their dignity, they will lash out at all around them in an attempt to fight back.

Their message may be, "If you will not like me, at least maybe you can respect me; and if you cannot respect me, at least you will fear me. I am a force to be reckoned with, if only a force of destruction and hostility."

Even in the case of recalcitrant criminals, it is worth our time to try to deal with the pain that lies hidden beneath the surface of their violent anger.

Recidivism. The time has come to admit that our present criminal justice system is more a failure than a success. The recidivism rate stands near 70 percent, and the incidence of violent crime is increasing. What exists is achieving neither deterrence nor rehabilitation.

The time is at hand for our best minds to be put to the task of creative thinking on the matter.

The Christian Response

Reformation. Prison Fellowship is one agency that has been successful with some of their programs, the result of their creative experiments in prison reform. A recent episode in Atlanta was heralded by the press as a courageous and hopeful step.

Restitution. The experimental project focused on producing a model of restitution to implement a biblical principle of justice. The project enlisted help from civic organizations and local churches.

A part of the experiment included visiting the home of an elderly blind widow who had been a victim of theft twice in the previous year. She lived in poverty, enduring the winter months in a home that had no insulation. As a double victim of crime, she was selected to be the beneficiary of the experiment.

Reconciliation. Local tradesmen donated about $5,000 worth of insulation and other building materials. Several inmates from a Florida prison were then selected to be given two weeks of release time to act as a work team to winterize the woman's house. An esprit de corps developed among the men as they went to work, maneuvering on their stomachs in the crawl space beneath the house and affixing caulking material and weather stripping to the windows.

Respect. In two weeks, the home was completely winterized and the woman was overwhelmed by the kindness of the men. She spoke of them as "family," for love was exchanged as well as restitution given. The prisoners left with a sense of pride for a job well-done rather than feeling their customary sense of shame.

THE DIGNITY OF THE VICTIM

The Value of the Victim

The matter of restitution raises the other side of the criminal justice coin: the question of the value of the victim. So much legislation has been passed to protect the rights of the criminal that victims are feeling lost in the shuffle.

The issue of the humiliation of the rape victim in a public trial is a well-documented matter. What of the victim of the robbery, the mugging, the vandalism or the slander? Little attention is given to these people and the scars they bear.

The cycle is common. When a serious crime occurs, it

receives front-page coverage. The victim's name and, perhaps, picture are prominently displayed in the newspaper or on the evening news. Feelings of compassion are felt for the victim as his or her plight is made public.

But the old adage, "There is nothing more dull than yesterday's newspaper," soon makes its impact felt. What continues to be newsworthy are the events of the criminal's trial. Once the trial begins, the criminal moves into the spotlight, and his fate becomes the chief concern of the public.

The Plight of the Victim

With each day of the trial, the criminal's plight becomes more prominent, while the victim's plight recedes into the background to be forgotten. Even when a conviction ensues, the matter of restitution is often overlooked. Such ethical issues that emerge in a criminal investigation and trial were touched on brilliantly in the poignant film *Absence of Malice.*

THE DIGNITY OF THE POLICE

Sometimes lost in the concern for the criminal and for the victim is the plight of the community law enforcement officer. Since the turbulent era of the '60s, the image of the policeman has suffered.

Placed by Public in Adversary Role

Endures Ridicule and Hostility. The respected, smiling civil servant who stops traffic with the wave of a white-gloved hand while using the other hand to motion a schoolchild to cross the street has been consigned to the museum of Norman Rockwell magazine covers.[2] Now the policeman is known pejoratively as the "fuzz" or the "pig."

I remember the identification I felt with the author of a well-known book in Holland entitled *An Irishman's Difficulty with the*

Dutch Language. The book cataloged the humorous errors an English-speaking person makes when he tries to master the exotic language of the Dutch.

The most humorous episode of the book reported the trouble the Irishman encountered when he addressed a Dutch policeman by a "title" he learned while listening to his Dutch friends talk about police. He politely smiled at one officer and said, *"Dag, smeris!"* which is like you or me walking up to an American policeman and saying, "Hi, pig!"

To liken the police officer to a rooting hog in a muddy sty is to insult his dignity as a human being. To proliferate the insults only hardens the adversary posture that is developing between segments of the public and the police.

Experiences Frustration and Ingratitude. Though frequently perceived as an officer of power, the role of the law enforcement officer is still that of the public servant. His task is frequently frustrating as well as dangerous. For his is a low-paid, high-risk job that is made more difficult when he is made the target of public ridicule and hostility.

So the men in blue are becoming bitter, and their cries are being heard in novels and in protest marches. Behind their bitterness lies a frustration stemming from the failure of the courts to stand behind their arrests and an anger growing out of what the police perceive as a feeling of ingratitude from the public they serve.

Shamed by Incidents Of Police Misconduct

Of course, real incidents of police brutality do take place. "Overkill" does occur where unnecessary force is used in making arrests. And still unresolved racial overtones are clearly present in some such incidents.[3]

I had a frightening moment myself with an arrest scene in Mississippi. My wife and I were sleeping in our motel room when I was harshly awakened by a racket outside our window. I heard someone yell and a sound of metal clanging against the asphalt driveway.

As I looked outside, I saw a terrified black man spread-eagled across the trunk of my car and a policeman pressing the man's head down against the car with the barrel of his service revolver. The policeman's face was contorted with rage as he screamed, "Make one move, Nigger, and I'll blow you away."

When people are held in low esteem and their property is not honored, crime increases, and the lifeblood of the entire community is infected by the virulent disease of indignity.

Against the protests of my wife, I rushed outside to let the officer know I was watching the scene, as I was afraid he was going to "waste" the thief on the spot. With my emergence from the room, the policeman eased the pressure on the gun and proceeded to handcuff the man. Minutes later, squad cars arrived to take the man into custody. I was glad the man had been apprehended while engaged in helping himself to my hubcaps but I was even more relieved to be spared the vision of a cold-blooded murder.

I had an opportunity to speak with the arresting policeman the following day, and he explained to me that his tone of voice and threatening gestures were all part of normal apprehension procedure and were carefully contrived to intimidate the suspect into a cowering acquiescence. He explained that he had been completely under control and had no intention of shooting the man.

I wonder if he could still have explained his actions to me in quite that same way were he to have seen his own face in a mirror at the time of the arrest incident. If ever a man looked like he wanted an excuse to pull the trigger, he was it. His arrest technique may well have been an act, but if so it was a performance worthy of an Academy Award.

Caught in Difficulty of Arresting and Protecting

The business of law enforcement is difficult in the best of circumstances. Progress has been made in establishing policies restricting the use of forcible restraint. But making arrests is not a children's game, and the process is fraught with peril.

The line between protecting the officer and protecting the suspect is a thin one. Two human beings are involved here, both worthy of respect and dignity. We may rejoice at least in this: that we do not live in a totalitarian society where the very presence of a policeman is enough to incite terror.

JUSTICE WITH DIGNITY

The prison is a symbol of the ugly presence of evil in our world. "Crime" is the word we use for acts of violence against people and property. Insofar as it is an abstraction, it is a euphemism.

The Issue in Criminal Justice

At issue in criminal justice is the basic dignity of a person and his property. There is no such thing as a victimless crime, for in any crime someone or someone's property is violated.

In some crimes, only the perpetrator is harmed—but there is still a victim: the perpetrator himself. For he, too, is a person.

The impact of the assault against person and property affects a broad cross section of a society. Consider the following partial list of people drawn into play when a crime is committed:

Law enforcement officers	Court administrators
Medical professionals	Accountants
Hospital personnel	Clerks
Paramedical personnel	Prison administrators
Insurance agents and claims adjustors	Prison guards
Private investigators	Social workers
Lab technologists	Parole officers
Criminologists	Bondsmen
Ecclesiastical institutional personnel	Defense lawyers
Judges	Prosecuting attorneys

When people are valued and their property respected, crime decreases. When people are held in low esteem and their property is not honored, crime increases, and the lifeblood of the entire community is infected by the virulent disease of indignity.

For Further Reflection

1. How does the issue of capital punishment relate to the question of human dignity?
2. How were criminals treated under the Old Testament law?
3. What suggestions can you give to control the problem of homosexual rape in prisons?
4. What is the main purpose of a prison?
5. How do you define an unjust punishment for a crime?
6. Is torture of a prisoner ever justified? Why? Why not?
7. List ways the victims of crime can be helped.
8. What is the image of the policeman in your community?
9. What is the difference between retribution and restitution?
10. Do you think the present criminal justice system is equitable? Why? Why not?

DIGNITY IN THE CHURCH

T HE sector of society where we most expect to find the practice of the esteem of the person is in the Church. The Church exists as an institution designed to major in valuing people. However, it does not always work out that way.

People are often overlooked and neglected in this divinely ordained institution. The problem is compounded by the fact that people come to the Church with high expectations. When these expectations are not met, the disappointment can be severe.

I am frequently drawn into discussions about religion in settings involving secular meetings and seminars. Certain patterns emerge in these informal discussions. Many of the unchurched people tell me that they had once been church members.

When I ask them why they left the Church, the answers tend to be similar. They were not distressed by theological issues or church programs, rather, the accent is on broken relationships. They tell of having their feelings hurt by a remark from the minister or priest or of being slighted in some way by a clique in the Church. The issues that emerge are more sociological than theological.

I was asked by an elderly Methodist pastor, "What do you think the primary purpose of the Church is? Do you see the Church as an army or as a hospital?"

I thought the question strange, but I took the bait. Being a zealous seminary student at the time, I replied, "I suppose both dimensions have to be present, but I see the Church primarily as an army, mobilized by God with the mission of changing the world."

That concept is what excited me about the Church. The Church is called ultimately to be the "Church triumphant," and I knew that could not happen unless she were first the "Church militant."

The wise pastor looked at me sadly and said, "Son, unless the Church is first a hospital, it can never become an army."

To realize the import of what he was saying took me a few years.

Madalyn Murray O'Hair made the cynical comment, "The Church is the only army who shoots their own wounded." I think the comment is colored by the hostility toward Christianity that Mrs. O'Hair has made famous by her crusades for atheism.

I do not think the statement is true but, like most distortions, it borrows its effectiveness from the kernel of truth contained within it. I also wonder if Mrs. O'Hair was once a victim of a Church-imposed wound.

DISCIPLINE AND MERCY

Discipline as Part of Nurture

Examining the wounds people feel the Church has inflicted upon them, I know there are two sides to these tales of woe. The Church is called not only to a ministry of reconciliation (see 2 Cor. 5:18,19), but a ministry of nurture to those within her gates (see Eph. 4:11-32). Part of that nurture includes Church discipline (see 1 Cor. 5—6), which is not always taken kindly.

When people join a church they do so by taking specific vows about diligence in participation and support of the rest of the body. Not everyone takes those vows seriously.

I spoke with a man who was an active church member who became furious when he learned that his son had been dropped from the church's roll. He complained bitterly to me saying, "Isn't my son good enough to be a member here? Who do you people think you are passing judgment on him? If my son isn't good enough to be a member here, then neither am I and I will withdraw all my support from the church."

I tried to soothe the man's ruffled feathers and explain why the session[1] of the church had taken disciplinary action. The fact of the matter was that the son had not been to church for a single Sunday in over three years. He had completely neglected the sacraments and had not supported the church either with his time, talents, or money—all of which he had solemnly pledged to do.

The records showed that the man had been visited six times and was encouraged to become more active in the fellowship of the church. He had indicated clearly that he was no longer interested in the church and had no desire to be kept on the rolls as an active member. However, when he was dropped both he and his father were outraged. The father left the fellowship of the church still convinced that his son was the innocent victim of precipitous and unfair judgment.

Sensitivity as Part of Discipline

That membership requirements of most churches are less than that of the country club or the YMCA seems not to matter to some. The psychological weight of the church's censure is heavy, and people are sensitive about their status there. To be dropped from the church, no matter how justifiable the reasons are and how disinterested the party is, can be a crushing blow to the dismissed party.

God requires that such discipline be carried out in the church, but special sensitivity must be exercised when it is done. Even the most obstinate impenitence for heinous sin should not be treated with curt or preemptive dismissal. The discipline of the church is part of her priestly duty and must be carried out in a priestly manner if people are to be highly valued.

God Himself, like the prodigal's father (see Luke 15:11-32), lets people depart from Him when they are determined to go, but He lets them go with tears.

THE OLD TESTAMENT PROPHETS AND PRIESTS

Distinctions and Qualifications

In the Old Testament Church, a clear distinction existed between the role of the prophet and the role of the priest. The priests had a clearly-defined order with regularly assigned duties and functions. One had to be a Levite by birth to qualify for the priesthood.

The prophet did not qualify for his office biologically, but by special divine appointment. The prophet was individually called and gifted by God for a specific task. The prophet lived a lonely life, for his role as divinely commissioned critic was not a popular one.

Duties and Functions

The major difference between the role of the priest and the role of the prophet had to do with their speaking tasks. Both functioned as spokesmen, and both functioned as mediators. It was the function of the priest to speak to God in behalf of the people. It was the function of the prophet to speak to the people in behalf of God.

The priest ministered in the Tabernacle or Temple giving voice to the prayers of the nation and offering up sacrifices to God in the people's behalf. His task was to do those things that assuaged the wrath of God and bore the signs of reconciliation.

The prophet, on the other hand, was like a prosecuting attorney. The structure of the Old Testament Church was built around a covenant with legal stipulations attached to it. When the covenant-treaty was broken, a lawsuit was enacted.

When Israel broke her treaty with God, He pursued His people with a subpoena in the hands of the prophets. The prophet announced the judgment of God and delivered the oracle which called the nation to repentance. One Roman Catholic theologian described the function of the Old Testament prophet to be the "conscience of Israel."

THE NEW TESTAMENT PRIEST/PROPHET PASTOR

What significance does this Old Testament pattern have for the modern-day Church?

Most churches do not carry on a formal priesthood, and those that do, do not model it after the structures of the Old Testament Levitical order. Nor do we have divinely appointed prophets running around the desert (see Luke 1:80), giving inspired oracles of revelation or making ax heads float in the river (see 2 Kings 6:1-7). The days of Jeremiah, Elijah, and Isaiah are over, but our interest in them abides.

Continuing the Tasks

In spite of the fact that the modern Church reflects a new covenant, without a Levitical priesthood or canonical prophets, certain elements of the priestly and prophetic tasks continue. The Church is still called to pray and to offer the sacrifices of praise and honor to God. The Church is still called to speak God's word to the nation, exercising prophetic criticism to the culture. The order may change as well as the structure, but some of the most basic tasks of the ancient Church remain in force.

Combining the Offices

In the modern Church the roles of the priest and the prophet are not maintained by two separate and distinct offices. The roles are combined into the office of the pastor. The minister is expected to exercise both functions as he shepherds his flock.

When he leads the congregation in prayer, when he visits the sick and counsels the troubled, he is manifesting the priestly role. When he teaches the Scriptures and preaches the sermon, he is manifesting the prophetic role.

Balancing the Functions

Problems arise when these two functions get out of balance. Some pastors are drawn more to the prophetic aspect and others to the priestly aspect.

When a pastor exhibits a one-sided emphasis on the priestly, the people suffer from a lack of teaching and prophetic exhortation. When the pastor is unbalanced in the direction of the prophetic, the people get an excess of admonishment and very little encouragement. The biblical mandate is to both, and if there were a temporal priority to either, it would fall to the priestly.

Before a minister can be an effective prophet to his congregation, he must first be their priest. We tend to be closed to criticism from people who only admonish us and never minister to our pain. This principle applies not only within the congregation but especially to the Church's role in ministering to the local community.

MINISTERING TO THE LOCAL COMMUNITY

The accepted method of establishing a church has some flaws. We incorporate our congregation, build our sanctuary, and then put up a sign that says, "Welcome." The name of the church and its pastor are usually displayed on a sign outside of the church building.

Sitting Back and Waiting for the Wounded

It is almost like we hang out a shingle then sit back and wait for the needy to come to us. What a striking contrast to the ministry of Jesus who made it His business to go out of the way to search for the wounded and the outcasts of society. Where the pain in a community festers is where the Church should be.

Most tourists to Amsterdam remember their first view of the infamous red-light district of the city which boasts over 10,000 registered prostitutes, plying their trade under the full protection of the law. The district stretches several blocks along a canal which moves from the central station to the famous "dam" for which the city is named.

Strikingly, in this same area are venerable churches which boast a rich ecclesiastical heritage. In some cases, no more than five feet separates the church doors from the windows of the "stores" which display the colorfully bedecked professional women. Prostitutes loiter in the street, leaning against the door of the pastor's study.

When I saw the red-light district for the first time, I inquired of a native what the relationship was between the Church and these women. He replied that there was no relationship, as the two institutions politely ignored each other.

Or Going Out and Attending the Afflicted

I asked incredulously, "Doesn't anyone try to minister to these women?"

"Oh, yes," he replied, "the Salvation Army has a vital ministry going on here."

I then watched as an incongruous meeting took place. A young woman, wearing baggy, drab-blue clothes and with a bonnet tied around her head, entered the building where provocatively-dressed girls were advertising their goods to entice passing sailors. The occasion looked like a meeting between the eighteenth and twentieth centuries, as the workers from the Salvation Army sought out the girls trapped in white slavery.

The difference in that place between the Salvation Army and the organized Church is the difference between waiting for the afflicted to come to us and our making the necessary effort to go to them.

The Salvation Army is one of the few Christian organizations in Europe that enjoys the respect of the secular culture. Though the culture may reject the religious convictions of the Army, they are aware that when a crisis occurs and people are in pain, the Salvation Army is there. That kind of reputation is what the Church is supposed to have and will have when it takes its priestly task seriously in a community.

Planning Church Programs to Bring in the People

I spoke with a young Episcopalian priest who was assigned to a mission church in a depressed mill town in western Pennsylvania. He came to me asking how he could develop a program to bring growth to his small parish of 27 members.

When he identified his church as a mission church, I leapt to the conclusion that it had only recently been organized. As we discussed the strategy of new church planting, I asked him how long the mission church had been there.

I almost fell over when he replied, "About 70 years."

He went on to relate in pessimistic terms that his supervisor had told him it was unlikely his church would ever experience significant growth, as that is the pattern in depressed areas.

The young pastor looked at me and said, "Is there any way to get these people interested in the Church?"

Or Addressing Church Ministry to Needs of the People

I said, "From the perspective of church growth potential, you are sitting on a gold mine. It should be an easy matter to have your church bursting at the seams in a short period of time.

"Think of it. There are over 60,000 people living in your town. Sixty percent of those people do not belong to any church, and no one is ministering to their spiritual needs. That means you have over 35,000 potential new members from the untapped masses.

"You are also living in a community where there is enormous pain, where people are looking for someone who will care about them. The unemployment rate is staggering and the poverty level is severe.

"These are proud people, people who have labored in the steel mills and the coal mines since they or their parents arrived from the old country. They are not going to come crying to you about their pain. If you want to build a church you must go to them.

"Where will you find them? In three sites, you will find ready-made congregations who will respond to you, if you don't play games with them. Go to the bars, the union halls and the ethnic clubs, and you will find the unemployed congregated.

"Of course, they will be suspicious, but go where Jesus went and do what Jesus did and you will have your church. It may not be a rich church, but it will certainly be a vital one."

Unlike the rich young ruler of antiquity (see Luke 18:18-30), the man did not depart, shaking his head. He was genuinely excited about crossing the line to minister to the poor and needy of his town.

THE DIGNITY OF THE PASTOR

Not only the people need respect and loving care. More and more, pastors are being beaten down in terms of the diminishing respect accorded to their role. Watch the cartoon images of clergymen or the typecasting of the minister in the television drama.

Comic Stereotyping

The minister is depicted as somewhere between the clown and the buffoon. He is portrayed in the cartoons as the bald, overweight, inept country bumpkin. In the TV image he is the self-righteous, sanctimonious hypocrite.

Rarely do you see the minister depicted as masculine, godly, intelligent and articulate. Of graduate-level professionals, the clergyman is the lowest paid and least respected.

Qualified Respect

This caricaturing of the minister may seem strange in light of the fact that a modicum of respect still remains from former days for the high calling of the ministry. Ministers are still honored as leaders in the community. However, the honor and respect the minister receives, for the most part, is not from his socioeconomic peers.

He is treated kindly and frequently taken out to lunch by the men of the parish. And he is introduced to the banker's colleagues proudly as "my minister." He is given professional courtesies by the medical profession, discounts by the tradesmen and free outings to the country club for a game of golf.

Paternalistic Attitudes

However, he is still looked down upon by the successful businessman, the doctor and the attorney. The difference lies in the matter of attitude. What the minister often experiences from his peers is paternalism.

No one, the minister included, likes to be patronized; it is an insult to one's dignity. The benevolent slave owner showered his slave with kindnesses and benefits—as many a contemporary missionary has treated his cook/steward—but all the while he was calling him "boy."

False Assumptions

The minister is duly respected by his peers when he is in the context of his church, performing his duties as a pastor. But when he steps out into the "world," the attitude shifts. Here the assumption is that the pastor is helpless and naive, sheltered from the stark, unsavory realities of life, as if the pastor did not have to major in the results of these cruel realities every day.

Certainly, part of the problem between the pastor and his church is economic. Men who enter the ministry are not enticed to it for the financial reward it offers. The minister is prepared to live a life of financial sacrifice to fulfill his calling.

Yet, it is one thing for a person to choose a lower level of income and quite another that it be imposed upon him by others who consider him unworthy of higher compensation. Here the attitudinal problem affects the minister's self-esteem. When it is communicated to him that he is not worth much economically, he is human enough to feel the pangs of that judgment.

Clerical Distinctions

Admittedly, a few ministers pastor large, affluent churches and are spared the indignities borne by their less fortunate comrades of the cloth. And the pastor of a "bishopric" does enjoy the respect of his peers, as he finds himself at the head of a large "corporation." The patronage in these circumstances is usually passed down to members of the pastor's staff.

In the large church, where several members serve on the ministerial staff, a wide gap often exists between the respect afforded the senior minister and that given to his associates. In some churches, a distinction is made between an associate minister and an assistant minister. That distinction is generally lost on the people who refer to the associate minister as "the assistant minister." The distinction would not be lost, however, on the junior partner of a law firm who was accorded the status of a clerk.

The associate minister is not hired by the senior minister but by the congregation. The associate is usually a highly qualified veteran of the ministry who has special skills. The assistant, on the other hand, is a recent seminary graduate. It is

---

*No charlatan or demagogue, no one,
pious or profane, can destroy the dignity
which God has placed upon the pulpit.*

---

hard on the associate to have his years of competent service so lightly dismissed with a slip of the title.

Congregational Perceptions

However, in the people's eyes, if you are not the head man then you must be an assistant. Of course, any minister who is deeply bothered by all this is in the wrong profession. I mention it simply to heighten the awareness of the people, lest they unwittingly continue the insult.

Chances are the minister who suffers under this popular form of demotion has the grace never to mention it himself.

THE DIGNITY OF THE LAY LEADER

In most churches, in addition to the pastor and his paid professional staff, there exists some board or agency selected from the congregation to be the ruling body of the church. Sometimes these people are called deacons or elders or wardens or members of the consistory. In many cases they assume their positions by way of ordination.

Ordained, but Lay

Those who are ordained are sometimes miffed by being called "laymen." The term "lay" refers to the unordained, but it has come to mean "one who is not a seminary-trained paid professional."

Official, but Unrecognized

It is important for the spiritual life of the congregation that its officers get the respect and dignity worthy of their office. The Bible calls us to a special degree of respect and honor for those called out of the congregation to serve in special roles of leadership.

Often, however, the dignity due these offices is eclipsed by the central focus given to the minister. The minister is highly visible in the life of the congregation, while the work of the elder or deacon is more private. Frequently, the elders are visible only on special occasions, such as at the celebration of the Lord's Supper.

Named, but Unknown

Still, it is important for the people to know who their elders, deacons and vestrymen are. Everyone knows the name of the minister, but few can recite the names of the wardens or session members.

A small improvement could be made simply by listing the names of these people in the Sunday bulletin or by arranging a special place for them to be seated during the worship service, as some denominations have done with great success. The point is not to make a show of these people, but simply to enhance their respect that their office may receive the honor it deserves— and which God intended for the benefit of all the people.

THE DIGNITY OF THE MINISTRY

The Occupants of the Pulpit

The job of minister is a curious profession. It attracts all types of personalities to its ranks, drawing everything from the fervent zealot to the hardened cynic, from the true believer to the devil's advocate. Some seek the pulpit from a passion to win souls, others as a platform for teaching. Some are frustrated actors, looking for a stage on which to perform. Others are guilt-ridden neurotics, looking for an altar of atonement.

In the pulpit are men of anger preaching their own wrath as if it were God's and men of "compassion" voicing their own weaknesses. Among these clergy can be found conservatives and liberals; pietists and moralists; eloquence and monotony; fervor and platitude; exposition and opinion; accusation and confession.

We have pastors who are believers and pastors who are unbelievers. Some know God and others do not. Some enter the ministry out of a desire to prove to others that God does not exist or to justify their own unrighteousness.

Over two centuries ago, Gilbert Tennent[2] warned of "The Dangers of Unconverted Ministry." It created a furor at the time but spoke nothing new. The clergy murdered Christ, and the ministers stoned the prophets.

The Power of the Pulpit

A power resides in the pulpit. Where else can a man move into town and assume a position of leadership and authority overnight? Where else can we gain the attention of a group week after week to hear our views uninterrupted?

The pulpit is a strange institution, sometimes filled with hypocrisy and unbelief, but God has chosen the foolishness of it all to save the world. No charlatan or demagogue, no one, pious or profane, can destroy the dignity which God has placed upon the pulpit.

THE BISHOP: BIBLICAL MODEL OF THE PASTOR

The pastor serves as a mirror image of the New Testament bishop. He may not hold the rank of the ecclesiastical position but he shares in the vocation. The word "bishop" comes from the Greek *episcopus*, from which the English word *episcopal* derives.

The Chief Executive

The root is the word *scopus* which is carried over into the English as "scope." In its ordinary sense, the word does not refer to a brand of mouthwash, but to an instrument used for sight. We think of the telescope, the microscope, and if we have ever suffered from hemorrhoids, the proctoscope.

Its Latin equivalent is *supra-videre* from which we get the word *supervisor*. Both visor and scope call attention to looking at something with the prefix adding a degree of intensity.

In the Greek world, a bishop was an official responsible for inspecting military troops to examine their combat readiness. He was like the visiting general who appears unannounced at the military outpost to review the troops. He was like the health inspector, the safety inspector or the quality control inspector who drops in unexpectedly to review our performance. The title was also applied to choirmasters who had the task of blending the individual voices of the choristers into melodious harmony.

The Good Shepherd

In the New Testament, the word *bishop* is used not only for a church officer but also as a title for both Christ and God the Father. When used for Jesus, it is joined with the title Shepherd, as Christ is both Bishop and Shepherd of our souls (see 1 Pet. 2:25, *KJV*). What is true of the characteristics of the Good Shepherd (John 10:11,14) may be applied to the characteristics of the good bishop.

Knowing the Sheep Individually. Chief among those characteristics is that the good shepherd knows his sheep (see John 10:14). I have often wondered about that as, I have never been a shepherd nor looked closely at the behavior of sheep. To me, sheep look so much alike; if you have seen one sheep, you have seen them all.

But I have been involved in raising dogs and am aware that a litter of puppies seems, at first glance, to be a mass-production of carbon copies. Soon, however, each member of the litter begins to display its own idiosyncrasies and character traits. Each has its own temperament and each responds to the trainer in slightly different and distinctive ways.

The trainer must mark these subtle differences to be effective in his job. This may or may not be true of sheep, but it is undoubtedly true of people.

The funeral service when my father died was not an event I looked forward to. In times of grief, our senses are numbed to what is going on around us and recollections tend to be fuzzy. But one aspect of this funeral service stands out vividly in my memory.

During the eulogy, the minister of our church made passing mention of my father's style of walking. He remarked that when my father came to the church, the minister knew it was my father approaching "by his footfall."

After the funeral I asked my mother about this remark which puzzled me. I was not aware of any distinctive characteristic to my father's gait, as he neither limped nor shuffled.

My mother's eyes, weary from tears of grief, began to sparkle as her face broke into a knowing smile. "Yes, your father did have a certain style of walking that was just a part of him. I knew exactly what the minister was referring to, and I was surprised that he was aware of it."

My mother was deeply moved by the mention of a subtle trait that was part of her intimate knowledge of her husband. I was impressed, because the minister had a congregation of over 2,000 members, and that he would know their idiosyncrasies was more than I could imagine. In this moment of family grief, he touched a tender nerve because he took the time to get to know his people.

Serving the Sheep Selflessly. Another characteristic Christ attributed to the Good Shepherd was the Shepherd's willingness to lay "down his life for the sheep" (John 10:11, *NIV*), a sharp point of contrast with the hireling shepherd (vv. 12,13). If the sheep tended by the hireling were attacked by wild animals, the hireling took no chances with his own safety, being unwilling to take risks for the benefit of his flock. But if the sheep of the Good Shepherd were attacked, He put Himself between the attacker and the sheep.

If a sheep was lost in dangerous terrain, the hireling made no attempt to recover it. But if the Good Shepherd's sheep were lost, He searched until he found it (see Matt. 18:12,13; Luke 15:3-7). His theme song was not "leave them alone and they'll come home wagging their tails behind them."

The Dignified Leader

As a Bishop of men, Christ was acquainted with the pangs of leadership. He shared the loneliness of the chief executive office and the hassle of a disgruntled work force. He endured the internal wrangling and jealous rivalries of associates competing to get close to Him.

His hard decisions were made in solitude and He was constantly misunderstood by subordinates. His yoke was easy, yet His students grumbled under it. His directives were challenged and His team second-guessed Him.

His closest friends betrayed Him and, in His darkest hour, fell asleep on the job. His motives were impugned and His dignity assailed by the very people for whom He sacrificed. He did all these things and did them to perfection.

Wonder ye then at the fiery trials of pastors less gifted and leaders less noble?

If any man ever earned the right to adopt an adversary style of leadership, cracking down hard on ungrateful subordinates, it was Jesus of Nazareth. But His legacy was not the model of the martinet nor the example of the imperious tyrant. He was a bishop who set the standard for dignified leadership.

The Ministering Visitor

The Bible also uses the term *bishop* as a designation for the work of God the Father. The usage is normally found in its verb form rather than its noun form. The Old Testament speaks of a common motif among the Jews, an expectation of the coming "day of visitation of the Lord."

This "Day of Visitation" took on both positive and negative overtones for Israel. The visitation of God was both a time of judgment and a time of redemption. God visits for two reasons:

First, He comes like the Greek *episcopus* to review the troops and evaluate their state of worthiness. This is the frightening aspect of the image. The prophets speak of the day when God will appear and find the people disobedient.

Amos, for example, warns the people of Israel that the day of the Lord is a day of darkness, there is no light in it (5:18,20). The same notion is found in the New Testament with reference to the future return of Christ (see 1 Thess. 5:1-3) It will be a moment of crisis for those who have ignored Him.

Second, for those who have been faithful to God, enduring the disdain of this world while remaining steadfast in their loyalty to Him, the day of visitation is a glorious time of vindication (see 1 Thess. 5:4-11). The day of visitation has the characteristics of a two-edged sword, bringing grief and misery to some, and felicity to others. The difference rests with one's diligent preparation for it.

The word translated "visit" is the verb form of the noun *bishop*. When God visits His people, the text may be rendered literally that God "bishops" His people. The verb form appears in the New Testament song of celebration by Zechariah, the father of John the Baptist: "Blessed be the Lord God of Israel, for he

---

We are to exhibit a form of behavior and attitude...that will mirror...the compassion of Jesus.

---

has visited and redeemed his people, and has raised up a horn of salvation for us in the house of his servant David" (Luke 1:68,69, *RSV*).

The incarnation of Christ is the acme of the visitation of God. His earthly work embodies the Father's role of the divine Bishop. From elements of His ministry, the ecclesiastical bishop takes his cue.

The bishop is to practice a kind of imitation of Christ on earth; not in the sense that the earthly bishop can *effect* man's redemption but in the sense that he can apply it and bear witness to it. This is what Martin Luther had in mind when he declared that it is the duty of every Christian to "be Christ to his neighbor."

None of us could qualify to be Christ in an ultimate sense, but we are to exhibit a form of behavior and attitude toward other people that will mirror for them the compassion of Jesus. Fairly or not, people do read that mirror and base their verdict of Christ on what they see there. To some, the Christian exudes the sweet-smelling savor of redemption, but others despise Christ because of us.

A primary ministerial duty in the Church is the practice of the "pastoral call." Home and hospital visitation is a routine part of the minister's job. This ministry takes its point of departure from the divine pattern of visitation.

Unfortunately, some visits are perfunctory with the time spent discussing the weather and local events. The intended function of the pastoral call is to minister to the needs of the people. Here the pastor has the opportunity to get to know his people, to become aware of their strengths and weaknesses; to bring the admonishment and consolation of God where it is needed.

Christ established a priority in the care of orphans and widows. The visitation of the sick and imprisoned is declared to be of the essence of true religion. When a person is visited, he is assured that someone cares about him. When the person is left unvisited, contrary feelings are stirred up and the person is left to think that no one cares about him. A frequent complaint of elderly church members, particularly among the legions of the widowed, is that no one ever comes to see them.

THE CHURCH AND STATE CRISIS

The Church's Ministry to the Secular Culture

The Church has a ministry, both priestly and prophetic, to the secular culture in which it is found. When the Church is priestly in her mission, her touch of mercy is often welcomed. But when the Church seeks to be prophetic in the secular culture, a howl of protest is heard from those clamoring about separation of Church and state, protesting that the Church has no voice outside its own domain.

M. Stanton Evans, publisher of *Consumer's Research Magazine* and a nationally known writer and columnist, spoke to this issue:

For those who study the history of our country and the current perils that beset it—that theme is incontestably correct. For openers, there is the fact that America was founded on religious principles, many interwoven with the civil institutions of the states.

The point of the First Amendment ban against a national established church was to protect such state and local religious practices, not to destroy them. Secular liberal doctrine on this issue has stood the Constitution on its head.

This topsy-turvy reading of fundamental law is part of a long-running war against religious principle in America.[3]

The Secular Revision of the First Amendment

The First Amendment has indeed been turned on its head in a topsy-turvy game. A subtle but devastating twist of logic has turned the concept of separation of church and state into separation of God and state.[4]

The Separation of God and State. The original concept of the amendment, while guaranteeing religious freedom of expression in every sphere of life, also distinguished between the spheres of authority of the Church and the state as functioning institutions. For instance, the Church's role is not to levy taxes or raise a standing army, nor is the state's role to baptize or ordain the clergy.

The Denial of God Altogether. Both the Church and the state were considered to be under God, recognizing the Creator's sovereign authority over His entire creation. To separate state and God, therefore, is to deny God altogether. For a God who has authority only over the sphere of the Church is finite, bound by space and time—no God at all, merely a creaturely idol.

The Church's Mandate to Speak Prophetically

The Church must speak her prophetic voice, addressing the ethical issues of the land. It is her constitutional right and her divine mandate. To strip the Church of this sacred right and duty is to put her in a ghetto, deifying the state as the autonomous voice of authority. That is precisely the totalitarian role of the state the Constitution was written to prevent.

The Sacred Necessity of Civil Disobedience

If the secular revision of the First Amendment prevails, the Christian will face the sacred necessity of civil disobedience. Christ will not permit His people to remain huddled in fear in an upper room, safely secure from a hostile empire. If we refuse to open the doors, He will break them down and push us through them to be priests and prophets to an aching land.

FOR FURTHER REFLECTION

1. Do you have friends who have dropped out of church because of hurt feelings? What can you do to help them?
2. How would you describe the main tasks of the Church?
3. Does the Church have the right to discipline its members? Why? Why not?
4. What do you think of excommunication?
5. Is your church oriented more to the priestly or the prophetic aspects of ministry?
6. How can your church be more priestly? More prophetic?
7. Where are the pockets of pain in your community?
8. What is the image of the clergy in your community?
9. List ways you can enhance the esteem of your pastor.
10. List ways you can enhance the esteem of your church officers.

CHAPTER NINE

The Marxist Option

THE history of the world was dramatically altered by a labor
movement which took place over 3,000 years ago. History's
biggest strike occurred in Egypt when a slave-labor force
walked off the job and left the country. It was called the Exodus.

A Classic Case of Economic Oppression

The Dispute
The dispute which gave us Moses and the nation of Israel centered on economic oppression. It was an economic crisis of the
highest magnitude. The sinister roots of the problem are outlined
in narrative history:

> Now there arose a new king over Egypt, who did not
> know Joseph. And he said to his people, "Behold, the
> people of Israel are too many and too mighty for us.
> Come, let us deal shrewdly with them, lest they multi-

ply, and, if war befall us, they join our enemies and fight against us and escape from the land." *Therefore they set taskmasters over them to afflict them with heavy burdens* (Exod. 1:8-11, *RSV*, italics added).

The Oppression

Oppressive supervisors were the tools used by a ruthless Pharaoh to enslave a nation. It was a cold-blooded act of tyranny, calculated to prevent the labor force from the freedom of leaving the land for new work opportunities. It was the ancient world's version of the Berlin Wall and the martial law of Poland.

We read further.

> So they made the people of Israel serve with rigor, and made their lives bitter with hard service, in mortar and brick, and in all kinds of work in the field; in all their work they made them serve with rigor (Exod. 1:13,14, *RSV*).

Harsh quotas were established by Pharaoh for the making of bricks. The foremen enforced the quota system with whips. To aggravate the misery of the slaves and to trim the cost of overhead, Pharaoh decreed that management would not supply the straw necessary for producing the bricks. "I will not give you straw. Go yourselves, get your straw wherever you can find it; but your work will not be lessened in the least" (Exod. 5:10,11, *RSV*).

One Israelite was enraged by the mistreatment of the workers and, in a fit of anger, murdered a foreman. His was not murder in the first degree. There was no premeditation, no malice aforethought. His was a murder in the heat of passion, but murder nonetheless, making it necessary for him to flee into the desert and live out his life as a fugitive.

Decades later the fugitive, now stooped with age, his face

made of leather from the desert sun, met God in the midst of a bush that burned but was not consumed. From the midst of the fire came a voice, "I have seen the affliction of my people who are in Egypt, and have heard their cry because of their taskmasters; I know their sufferings" (Exod. 3:7, *RSV*).

The fugitive was sent by God to deliver a message to Pharaoh. The message was terse and unambiguous: "Let my people go" (5:1).

The Walkout
When Pharaoh let God's people go, they went and became a great nation, rising to the level of a world power under the leadership of David, their greatest king. But their golden era was brief, as the kingdom soon divided and plunged into bloody civil war. Then followed a succession of corrupt kings whose administrations were marred by court intrigue and oppressive policies. The nation grew so weak that it finally fell; the people were led away once more to a burdensome captivity.

The Moral
The seeds of Israel's destruction were sown in the same manner they had known in Egypt. David's famous son, Solomon, known for his wisdom, celebrated for his wealth and administrative skills, was the one who sowed the bitter seeds. He got carried away with his building projects, enslaving his own people as his private labor force. The world's wisest man became a stupid ruler.

In our world today, Pharaohs and Solomons can still be found. They are the rulers who think economy can be improved by oppressive tactics, the tyrants who rule by the whip and by unreasonable quota systems. There are also the fools who, echoing the words of Pharaoh, say, "God has no place in economic issues."

Such men should be careful to avoid burning bushes.

THE MARXIST IMPACT

Nearly as ancient as the brain-twisting query of the chicken and the egg is another question of temporal sequence. The question is, Do ideas shape events or do events shape ideas?

We can soften the dilemma a bit by answering, "Both." Since no philosopher ever operates in a historical vacuum, we have some sense in which events shape ideas.

The realities of the present are the spawning ground for fertile ideas. At the same time, the seminal ideas of the present are capable of germinating new forms and structures for the future. We find that a reciprocal tension oscillates between idea and event, and event and idea.

The impact of philosophy upon a culture is usually slow and gradual. It begins with a tedious scholar like Plato, Aristotle or Kant composing a technical tome which only a few learned professors understand in its initial presentation.

Later the complex ideas are grasped and employed in the media of the art world, being communicated to a broader audience through the novel, the painting, the film or the sculpture. From that level, it passes to the popular media until it impacts the masses. By the time the "new" philosophy reaches the popular level, it is usually outdated in the scholarly world.

To think a philosophical theory could radically alter the daily lives of 2 billion people in a time frame of less than a century is to push the anticipatory powers of the mind to the limit. Yet that is precisely what has happened in the last century with the impact on the world of the philosophy of Karl Marx (1818-1883).

The Preoccupation with the "Red Peril"

It was easy to be jaded with the hysteria of the '50s by our nation's preoccupation with the issue of the "Red Peril." The McCarthy[1] era left a sour taste in the mouth of a public made to swallow the bitter pills of that time. Vivid reminders of the spread of communism were ubiquitous, from the senate hearings to the popular television series, "I Led Three Lives," based on the counterespionage activities of Herbert Philbrick. Daily warnings were issued to the American public from the somber office of America's then number one G-man, J. Edgar Hoover.[2]

One can sustain an atmosphere of alarmism only so long. A moment of quietude must come when the sirens cease their wailing and the "all clear" is sounded. Once McCarthy was discredited, the Berlin Blockade[3] ended and the Korean conflict[4] ground to a halt, a new advent of happy days arrived and the nation was able to return to business as usual.

The Countermood of Skepticism

A countermood of skepticism set in by which no one wanted to be caught in the vortex of a new wave of Red hysteria. I, for one, was saturated with alarmism and negatively impressed by those who still insisted on searching for communists behind every bush.

I was roused from my dogmatic slumber by an academic alarm clock. As a student of philosophy and theology, I was required to examine the thought of Karl Marx to round out my understanding of the history of Western thought. My graduate studies were done in Europe where I discovered a different breeding ground for the birth of radical ideas.

The Debate over Economic/Political Systems

Europe in the '60s was still depressed from the ravages of World War II, and the debate over preferred economic and political systems was very much alive. Particularly the younger generation of students exhibited keen interest in the thought of Karl Marx.

A strong anti-American sentiment was directed mainly against the "rich cousin" who was accused of reducing Europe to a state of economic slavery. The resentment was often fierce, and some young thinkers gave allegiance to European strands of Marxism as a viable alternative to Yankee imperialism.

In the theological halls of Europe, the prevailing fashion of intellectual fad was to create a synthesis between dimensions of Marxist theory and classical Christianity. It would be years before that new synthesis was transported across the Atlantic to penetrate the American seminaries under the rubric of Liberation Theology.

The Reawakening to Realities of Marxism

A popular reawakening to the realities of Marxism hit the United States at the close of the '70s and the beginning of the '80s. The specter of Afghanistan[5] in 1979, followed closely by the 1980 Solidarity crisis in Poland,[6] alerted the nation to a new juggernaut of Marxist expansion. The influence of Karl Marx had not diminished but was growing in force and spreading like a cancer over the earth.

The Advent of *Glasnost* and *Perestroika*

From Joseph Stalin through the administration of Leonid Brezhnev, the USSR imposed Marxism and dominated governments in eastern Europe, Asia, Latin America and Africa more fully than had any previous colonial power or empire. Then in March 1985, Mikhail Gorbachev, the youngest member of the Politburo, was chosen General Secretary of the Communist Party. His leadership style and attitude quickly indicated that his country and the world were in for some major changes, the scope and direction of which remained to be seen.

The changes were not long in coming. Gorbachev soon initiated a program of national reforms that allowed for expanded freedoms and a democratization of the political process. He spoke of *glasnost* (openness) and *perestroika* (restructuring).

A stunned, but cautious free world cheered and welcomed these developments, but the enthusiasm was not universal. Many old-line communists within the USSR and entrenched Marxist governments in the eastern bloc countries resisted any loosening of the system that had empowered them and enslaved the people. But the promise of new freedoms was both intoxicating and contagious, and people everywhere caught the fever.

Poland. By mid-1989, following some 10 years of destabilization brought about by the Solidarity labor movement, Poland already had a noncommunist government in power. It came about on June 4, when Solidarity-endorsed parliamentary candidates were swept into office during the country's first free elections in 40 years. And, on August 19, 1989, Tadeusz Mazowiecki became prime minister and the first noncommunist to head an eastern bloc nation.

Hungary. In Hungary, on October 18, 1989, the National Assembly amended the constitution to prepare for free multiparty elections in 1990. The Assembly also removed references in the constitution to a leading role for the Communist Party, ending the party's power monopoly. Five days later, on October 23, Acting President Matyas Szuros proclaimed Hungary a free republic.

Germany. In then East Germany, the government of President Erich Honecker adamantly opposed the USSR's new policy of *glasnost,* but nationwide demonstrations forced Honecker's resignation, also on October 18, 1989. Events then moved quickly. In the first week of November, the border with Czechoslovakia was opened and citizens were permitted to travel to the West.

A few days later, on November 9, the border with West Germany was opened. The Wall separating the two Germanys was breached at last after 28 long years. Reunification soon followed on October 3, 1990 and the first all-German elections since 1933 were held on December 2.

Czechoslovakia. In Czechoslovakia, on November 17, 1989, massive anti-government demonstrations took place in Prague, as tens of thousands of protesters demanded free elections. A week later, the Communist Party leadership resigned and a nationwide strike ensued. On December 10, less than a month since the protests had begun, a cabinet without a Communist majority took power for the first time in 41 years. Vaclav Havel, a leading civil rights campaigner, was chosen president on December 29.

In his 1990 New Year's Day address to the people of Czechoslovakia, President Havel, looking back, said:

> Notions such as love, friendship, compassion, humility and forgiveness have lost their depth and dimension....The previous regime, armed with its arrogant and intolerant ideology, denigrated man into a production force and nature into a production tool....It made talented people who were capable of managing their own affairs...into cogs in some kind of monstrous, ramshackle, smelly machine whose purpose no one can understand.[7]

Romania. In Romania, the handwriting was already on the wall. On December 16, 1989, the country's hard-line government ordered troops to fire on protestors demonstrating in Timisoara. Hundreds were killed and buried in mass graves.

As protests spread elsewhere, Communist President Nicolae Ceausescu declared a state of emergency. But the rebellion continued and, by December 21, it had spread to Bucharest. Again security forces were ordered to shoot down protesters.

Instead, many army units joined the rebellion, and by the next day a "Council of National Salvation" declared itself to be in power. Ceausescu and his wife fled, but were captured on December 23. Quickly tried and found guilty of genocide, they were executed December 25.

The Baltic States. Meanwhile, in the USSR, ethnic and

nationalist unrest developed in the 15 Soviet republics with almost all of them agitating for increased autonomy and possibly for full independence. The Baltic states of Estonia, Latvia and Lithuania were in the forefront of those seeking release from the grip of the Soviet Communist Party upon them. Resistance came in the form of both bullets and ballots.

The recent experience of the republic of Lithuania may be a portent of the future for all the Soviet republics. On December 7, 1989, it was the first of the republics to vote for the adoption of a multiparty political system, removing from the republic's constitution articles guaranteeing the Communist Party a monopoly on power. In another unprecedented action, the Lithuanian Communist Party, on December 20, declared itself independent of the national party, stating that its goal was the creation of an independent democratic Lithuania.

Six days later, Gorbachev declared this action to be illegitimate and asserted that secession was out of the question for any of the Soviet republics. Nevertheless, in March 1990, the Lithuanian parliament voted unanimously for independence and followed this action by forming a noncommunist government. But in June, following Soviet intervention, Lithuania rescinded the declaration of independence.

Another Soviet military intervention also took place in January 1991. And Gorbachev announced subsequently that Lithuania's February 1991 referendum on independence for the republic—in which 90 percent of those voting favored independence from the Soviet Union—had no legal standing. He held instead a countrywide referendum in March 1991 on a possible Soviet federation of states. Though several republics boycotted that referendum, those which participated gave him a majority vote.

Those developments left Lithuania wondering how best to proceed on the road to full independence and whether any initiatives taken in that direction would necessarily be more symbolic than practical.

The Future of Capitalism in Europe

These various popular movements for autonomy and independence were fueled as much by genuine grievances as by the first taste of freedom. Soviet central planning had already proved itself a total failure. The nation could no longer feed itself, industrial production was all but paralyzed and empty stores confirmed that basic goods and services, the necessities of everyday living, were simply nonexistent.

By 1990, Gorbachev notwithstanding, the manifest inabilities of the Soviet system had already discredited communist ideology and had demonstrated beyond question the ultimate bankruptcy of communism when applied to the realities of life. Not surprisingly then, in March 1990, along with electing Gorbachev as the country's president and stengthening the power of that office, the National Parliament of the USSR repealed the provision in the Soviet Constitution that granted the Communist party a monopoly of political power.

As the world watches and Christians pray, the developments continue to unfold in the USSR, in its many republics and in its former satellite states.

The final outcome remains uncertain. Mikhail Gorbachev's grip on power is not total. Can he remain at the helm? And, if so, for how long?

Even if he stays in power, we dare not think of Gorbachev as a latter-day convert to capitalism. He remains, by his own admission, a committed communist, though he is more of a pragmatist and less of an idealogue than any of his post-Lenin predecessors.

In seeking to move the USSR from a centrally planned economy to a free-market economy, is Gorbachev determined to scrap the existing system or is he merely trying to reform it? Was he conceding the impossibility of going back to the old way of doing business when, in a rare admission to the Supreme

Soviet in September 1990, he declared, "The system is no longer there; it's gone"?[8]

The situation in eastern Europe remains in flux. New events unfold almost daily and circumstances change constantly. The best answer we can give right now on the ultimate significance of political and economic developments there is that the jury is still out.

The Threat to Capitalism in Europe

Perhaps the greatest threat right now to the future of capitalism in eastern Europe is the fact that the transfer of power in a society from communist rule to democracy does not automatically bring about an economy driven by the demands of the marketplace. How are the new democratically oriented leaders of these various countries to make the transition from a centrally planned economy to a free-market economy?

Poland attempted to make the transition in a single leap with an incredible escalation of prices for basic commodities. The cost of gasoline doubled, for instance, and the price of coal sky-rocketed 600 percent. Their radical reform effort succeeded, but it was undergirded by massive economic aid from the United States and West Germany, until prices settled back to normal levels and the economy stabilized.

The truth is that "in Eastern Europe, only the elderly had much recollection of the meaning and implementation of democracy and free-market economy. In the Soviet Union, with no relevant history at all, these concepts have no meaning. Therefore, despite some individual demonstrations of real statesmanship, the whole process of change seemed to some degree to be an exercise in which the blind were leading the blind."[9]

Inexperience, ignorance and ineptitude can prove as hazardous as ideology to the solid economic health and growth of a people.

MARX'S VIEW OF MAN

How do we understand Marxism? What are the core ideas that generate such far-reaching impact on the life of nations?

We would be simplistic to assume that what we know as modern communism is a rote application of classic orthodox Marxism, for Marxism comes in as many varieties as there are participants in the communist bloc. Marxist theorists debate among themselves as to what the essential ingredients of the philosophy are. Admittedly, without certain basic notions that are in the original work of Marx, communism would be unintelligible.

Important to note at the outset is the fact that Karl Marx was first a scholar before he experienced his baptism as a revolutionary. Some picture him racing across Red Square brandishing a sword or throwing a Molotov cocktail. A more accurate image would be to envision a nondescript student, huddling to keep warm in a corner of the British Museum in London. It was in that vast library that the real genius of the revolution was born.

Like most nineteenth-century students of philosophy, the young Marx was concerned with working through a philosophy of history. The chief interest in the schools had turned away from standard issues of metaphysics to focus on the dynamic movement of history. This new vista was sparked by the prodigious work of the century's premier philosopher, G. W. F. Hegel (1770-1831).

Hegel had constructed a complex system of thought in which history was understood as a movement of opposing ideas fleshing themselves out in the concrete arena of time and space. Ideas meet, clash and then merge into new ideas as the pattern of history moves on. Hegel's system was called *dialectical idealism,* a kind of abbreviated shorthand to capture the essence of his thought.

A New View of History

Though Marx was heavily influenced by the work of Hegel, he was not satisfied with some of its basic features. Marx agreed that history is propelled by a series of conflicts—of clashes and counterclashes. But he believed it is not the conflict of ideas that propels history, but the conflict of economic forces that bring about change. The material side of life makes history, not the spiritual or intellectual side. Hence Marx's system of *dialectical materialism* placed the conflict or "dialectic" in the material realm rather than in the realm of ideas.

A New View of Man

Marx departed from the traditional definition of man as *Homo sapiens*; Marx located the uniqueness of man in his labor. He defined man as *Homo faber* or "man the maker, the one who labors or fabricates."

This new designation for man fell like a bombshell on the philosophers' playground. Marx was dragging philosophy down from the ethereal plains of Hegel to the sweat and grime of the factory. The dynamic history of mankind is to be explained in terms of man as a laboring animal.

Later, critics of Marx complain that he was guilty of the cardinal sin of the philosopher, the sin of reductionism. It is a common temptation among creative thinkers, after discovering a new nuance of meaning, to use that isolated aspect to explain the whole. To reduce the whole meaning of human history to the clashes of human labor would involve an oversimplification of the complexity of man.

A New View of Labor

Whether Marx was guilty of such a reduction is unimportant. Regardless of his failures, philosophers since Marx have found it virtually impossible to define the meaning of man without taking into serious consideration the vital importance of human labor. Whatever else man is, he is a creature intimately related to his work.

According to Marx, the Industrial Revolution brought a crisis to *Homo faber*. The appearance of the factory (the *Fabriek*) brought upheaval to man's natural work patterns. Now, instead of enjoying the liberty of self-sufficient production whereby the farmer could meet his own needs by the toil of his labor, the working man became a kind of economic slave dependent on the capitalist for his survival.

The laborer in the factory was considered by Marx to be nothing more than a wage-earning slave. In this scheme, man's labor was divorced from himself, with someone else owning his labor. As a result, the working man suffered the crisis of estrangement from his nature.

THE DYNAMIC OF TOOLS

With the advent of capitalism, ownership was concentrated in the hands of the few. The key to the expanded production and enormous increase of material wealth generated by the Industrial Revolution was found in the sophistication of man's tools.

For Marx, the Archimedean levers of labor are the "means of production." The means of production translate simply into "tools." Whoever controls the tools, controls the game.

Modern anthropologists frequently fix the advent of man on the scene of history by the appearance of primitive tools. Often debated in the halls of paleontology is at what point humanoids cross the line to human beings.

Some fix the line of demarcation with the appearance of the instruments of labor. That is essentially what tools are—instruments to facilitate human work. Tools make it possible for men to increase their productivity.

The Possession of Tools

Consider, for example, the vast difference between the labor of a Columbian peasant and the production of a cotton farmer in Arizona. The two men may be of the same physical strength and mental capacity; yet the one ekes out a single bale of cotton in the same time required by the other to produce a hundred bales of cotton. The difference lies in the possession of tools.

We might add the following question: What happens to the price per unit of a cotton shirt in an environment where such shirts are mass-produced compared to the price of a shirt where they must be handmade one at a time?

The answer is simple and reveals the attractive quality of an industrialized society where the basic needs of human life such as clothes, shelter and food can be mass-produced for a cheaper cost.

The problem with tools is that not everybody can afford them. For that reason, the small farmer is vanishing from the rural scene of America. He cannot compete in the marketplace with the farmer equipped with a mechanized outfit of production.

Tools require initial capital to make their use possible. If one lacks the capital, he cannot obtain the tools. If he lacks the tools, he cannot compete.

If he cannot compete, he must submit himself to the status of working for someone else who does possess the capital to purchase the tools. Thus, says Marx, the independent agrarian worker is caught in the economic squeeze of capitalism and forced into the state of economic bondage.

A simpler version of the capitalistic squeeze is experienced by every boy involved in a neighborhood pick-up baseball game. Played without the benefit of formally sanctioned umpires, such ad hoc sporting contests frequently end in chaotic arguments about a disputed call of "safe" or "out." How are such neighborhood impasses resolved?

I know how it was done when I was a boy. The deciding ballot was always cast by the kid who owned the bat and ball. If you alienated the owner of the "tools," the ball game was over.

The Factor of Tools

A more complex and far-reaching dilemma of tools and economic competition may be seen in the current economic crisis facing the United States. As I am writing, our nation is caught in the throes of a severe problem of unemployment with two of our major industries struggling for survival. The automobile and steel industries are facing grave financial difficulties forcing mass layoffs and shutdowns across the nation.

On the surface, it seems unthinkable that foreign competitors could best American industries in their own backyard. How is it possible that a tiny nation like Japan, totally dependent on foreign imports for its raw materials, could produce an automobile, ship it across the Pacific Ocean, pay tariffs and still manage to undersell the local competition? Why are Japanese productivity rates spiraling, as our own are plunging to the lowest levels in our national history?

To answer these questions fully requires more knowledge than I possess. But certain factors that contribute to the situation are readily apparent even to the amateur economist. We know the Japanese worker holds no intrinsic physical or mental advantage over the American worker. And we know the Japanese people do not exceed the Americans in technological know-how.

Some have located the answers in lower Japanese labor costs, while others point to the higher level of worker morale in Japanese factories to explain their higher rate of productivity. As an advocate of the Value of the Person, I can only agree with the importance of these factors.

But another factor is there which is formidable—the factor of tools. In the nation of Japan, not an automotive factory is to be found that is older than 30 years. The *Japanese are competing with newer and better tools.* For various reasons, including high rates of taxation, American capitalism has fallen behind precisely at the pivotal point of capitalism, at the point of capital investment in newer and better tools.

The dynamic of tools and their ownership led Marx to the conviction that wealth was being divided in an unequal manner, reducing the masses to the level of slaves, estranging them from their own humanity. People are forced to sell their labor and abandon hope of retaining ownership in the fruit of their work. In capitalism, the wealth is accumulated by the owner; all others are slaves, albeit at different levels of slavery.

Marx did not foresee the emergence of the managerial class in capitalism or the strength that would emerge in the middle class. My guess is that the managerial class would fit in Marx's category of the proletariat.

Managers are merely upper-echelon slaves with a higher wage base than the laborer. What the manager lacks is ownership. The labor he sells may be more highly skilled than that of the hourly wage earner, but he is still playing with someone else's bat and ball.

MARX AND RELIGION

How do we account for the fact that so much wealth is concentrated in the hands of so few owners?

Why do the masses not rise in revolt and strip the owners of their tools?

Why are there not more spontaneous uprisings to stop this exploitation of the poor by the rich?

How do the rich maintain the status quo and keep the proletariat in line?

An Extended Analogy of a Building

In providing answers to the above questions, Marx embarks upon his hostile attack on religion in general and Christianity in particular. He explains this phenomenon of the power structure with the aid of an extended analogy drawn from the building industry.

Marx considers the economic structures of a society in terms of a building image. A house includes both a substructure or foundation and a superstructure. The superstructure is built upon the substructure which provides its support.

Substructure. For Marx, the substructure of a society is the economic base upon which the society is established. The substructure reflects the system by which the means of production are controlled. Thus, the economic base of a nation is the foundation for all of its life. Change the nature of the foundation and the building standing upon it will fall.

In America, the substructure is capitalism. Destroy capitalism and American culture will disintegrate. Without the foundation, the house cannot stand.

Superstructure. When we look at a building, what strikes our eyes is not the foundation, but the edifice itself. The external forms of a culture that are immediately visible are what Marx calls the superstructure. The superstructure includes the legal system, the moral codes, the religious beliefs and the value system of society. But these aspects of cultural life merely reflect the hidden economic substructure beneath them.

A Reversed Understanding of Culture

What is revolutionary about Marx's view? The normal method of understanding the shape of a culture is radically reversed. In the Western world, we are accustomed to thinking that our value systems and ideals determine what form our economic structures will take. Law will determine the nature of our commerce, commerce will not dictate the nature of our law.

This is, however, precisely the point of the Marxist critique. The facts of history, declared Marx, prove that the value systems of law, religion and politics are dictated by the economic base of the nation. The laws and religious ideals are made to conform to the stark realities of the economic base and then are used as a rational defense for that economic system.

Religion. The popular axiom attributed to Marx, but not original with him, is the assessment, "Religion...is the opium of the people."[10] What is meant is that man, in his frustrated state of estrangement, turns to religion for consolation. If he cannot experience economic freedom in this life, maybe there will be a glorious "Exodus" in the next life.

In this scheme, the capitalist becomes the dope peddler who must keep the dreams of the masses focused on the other world. Religion is useful to keep the slumbering giant of the proletariat asleep or in a torpid state so that he remains docile and manageable.

The ownership class has a vested interest in the preservation of religion. He feeds his worker religious hope for the future while laughing all the way to the bank.

The slave is pacified by promises of a better life across the Jordan, if he practices the religious virtues of peaceful obedience to his earthly master.

Law. Religion is not the only wall of the superstructure. Of equal importance to the maintenance of the economic substructure is the legal system. According to Marx, the *legal system of a given society will always reflect the vested interests of the ruling class.* Lady Justice will demurely remove her blindfold in the presence of a wealthy suitor. The owner will inexorably seek to consolidate his wealth by backing it with the power of the courts.

Marx's critique of religion and law is designed to expose

their role as foils in the hands of the ruling class. He wants to strip away the facade from the superstructure so the reality of the substructure may be laid bare. For authentic economic liberation to occur, not only must the building be torn down, but the foundation must be rooted up and cast away.

The Liberating Revolution of the Proletariat
The natural forces of the movement of history will bring the downfall of capitalism, but that process can be hastened by the intentional actions of men, climaxed by the revolution of the pro-

> *The Christian agenda for human dignity is not a revolution....We want change, but we choose the model of reformation rather than revolution.*

letariat. Hence, the agenda of the Marxist is the violent overthrow of the existing substructures of capitalist societies. History has borne witness to the fact that the dream of such revolutionary activity was not an idle one.

One of the pedantic facts we were required to memorize as school children was the total population of the world. According to the 1950 report, the world population stood at some 2.6 billion persons. Within three decades, the population almost doubled to 4.4 billion.[11] So until the late 1980s—when the Iron Curtain began coming apart at its seams—the staggering fact confronting us was that the population then living under communist rule was equal to the population of the entire world in 1950.

By Marxist standards, those statistics represented a multitude of people who had tasted the blissful tonic of "liberation." The quality of life enjoyed by these liberated millions, however, is hardly a matter of envy, as the price tag of the new egalitarianism has been exorbitant. Though the Berlin Wall was opened in November 1989 and subsequently torn down, much of the Gulag[12] remains an abiding symbol of a dream gone mad.

STRATEGY OF THE MARXIST

Revolution vs. Reformation

If one is concerned for labor peace, he must be alert to the strategy of the Marxist. The key target group for inciting the masses to revolution is the working class. They are the nonowners whom Marx depicts as the brutalized victims of the capitalist.

Prod the slumbering giant and he will throw off the chains of economic slavery. It is not by accident that the principal propaganda vehicle of the American Communist Party is a daily newspaper originally named *The Daily Worker*. Though the name has since been changed to *The Daily World*, the target group remains the same.

Some years ago, the city of Pittsburgh was treated to a colorful array of posters which appeared overnight on telephone poles, vacant walls and old buildings. The posters boasted brilliant red and yellow images of Mao Tse-tung, announcing a celebration in honor of the chairman. At the bottom of the poster, in fine print, was the caption *Donated by Labor.*

Inquiring into the source of the poster campaign, I discovered there was a well-organized segment within existing labor union structures that openly proclaimed their allegiance to Maoism. Leaders of the labor unions have struggled to contain the radical platforms of the disgruntled minority who have despaired of the route of collective bargaining and contract negotiations. These militant few advocate the violent overthrow of existing economic and political structures.

The Christian agenda for human dignity is not a revolution. Acutely aware of the inequities and evils infecting the present structures, we want change, but we choose the model of reformation rather than revolution.

Reformation seeks to work peaceably from within the existing structures, to implement changes that will improve the quality of human dignity. The Christian clashes with the Marxist, abhorring statism as a perilous solution to man's problem of labor.

Economic Equality vs. Economic Equity

Much in Marx's analysis of the forces of history is worthy of our attention, and the crisis of ownership is paramount. The biblical value system puts a premium on personal ownership. The Old Testament Jew was promised the possession of land as an integral part of his redemption.

It will not do to soften the implication of that truth by defining ownership in terms of state ownership which insured an equal participation of each citizen in the full benefit of the land. Such egalitarian notions simply do not exist in the Old Testament. The accent there is not on economic *equality* but on economic *equity*. Private ownership is the order of the day in biblical sanctions, but it is an ownership that is protected and maintained by justice and righteousness.

Policies of business or law that exploit, cheat or oppress the poor receive the judgment of God. The prophets thundered against the abuses of the wealthy class who misused their power to afflict the poor; but the prophets were reformers, not revolutionaries.

Private ownership was not to be thrown out for the sake of egalitarian redistribution of wealth. When the egalitarian state owns everything, no one owns anything.

The Chains of the State vs. the Chains of the Capitalist

The irony of Marxism is that it intensifies rather than alleviates man's estrangement from his labor. In the communist system, man exchanges the perceived chains of the capitalist for the real chains of the state. The most important difference is that the capitalist inevitably pays him higher wages and offers a higher standard of living.

As earlier noted, Marx did not anticipate the emergence of a large middle class as happened in the United States. The middle class was made possible by a broad participation in private

---

Who decides the value of the product?
Only one person can determine the real
value of a product for you, and that is you.
The customer determines the price tag.

---

ownership. The American dream of the individual's owning his own home was realized.

Participation in ownership of the factory was made possible to the small investor by the stock market. The wages earned by the worker were able to be transformed into property ownership through savings and investment. There remained a poor class of people, but their standard of living was considerably higher than corresponding groups in Europe.

The first generation of immigrants was not susceptible to the empty promises of the Marxist. Their alleged "slavery" in America was a form of economic and political freedom they were willing to die for. These people understood the elementary axiom that there is no political freedom without economic freedom—an axiom their progeny have frequently overlooked.

A Mess of Pottage vs. the Abuses of Capitalism
The word *capitalism* once conjured up visions of golden oppor-

232 / *The Marxist Option*

tunities for free men to improve their miserable lot in the state of nature. Hordes of people abandoned native soil, selling all they owned to book passage to a harbor graced by a molded woman with spiked headdress. Fleeing the caprice of kings, the potato famine or the inquisitor's rack, they migrated to a place made rich by a grand experiment.

Today, however, a number of people within the Church and without, consider capitalism an ugly word, and to them the lady of the harbor—her 1986 face-lift notwithstanding—stands in disrepute.[13] The evils of greed, wasteful consumption, racial prejudice, political graft and corporate exploitation have so embittered them that they prefer to trade the ills they have for others they know not of. The modern-day Esau stands poised to trade his birthright for a mess of pottage.

But such a blanket indictment ignores the fact that any political system, any economic structure is vulnerable to the infection of evil. As long as capitalism is entrusted to people, abuses will be found. But in itself it stands on a single premise—*the right of every man to own the fruit of his labor.*

Totalitarian Repression vs. Individual Rights

If one owns his wages, he is not a slave, as wages are nothing more and nothing less than certificates of exchange for real goods and services. In an industrial society, whether one works in manufacturing or in a service-oriented enterprise, the mind is as much of a tool as a combine machine or a photocopier and may be freely used for the increase of wealth.

In totalitarian nations, the free expression of the mind leads not to wealth but to imprisonment, as seen in the lives of the USSR's Aleksandr Solzhenitsyn and Poland's Lech Walesa—or even to death as seen in Beijing, China's Tiananmen Square.

THE DIGNITY OF PROFIT

Capitalism thrives on profit.

> *Without profit,* there is no way to increase the productivity necessary to meet the material needs of humanity. If one cares for the poor, he cannot at the same time despise profit.
>
> *Without profit,* production stagnates as the tools wear out, the factory closes and the ranks of the unemployed swell to the bursting point.
>
> *Without profit,* commerce is impossible.

Why?

The Foundation of Profit

Trade, the exchange of goods and services, rests on a foundation of profit. Without the desire for profit, no exchange will be made except by force, which we call theft.

Let us examine the matter in simple terms.

Suppose you are gifted at the making of shoes, and your neighbor is a farmer, gifted with an ability to grow food. You need food to eat, and your neighbor needs shoes to keep his feet warm. You produce more shoes than you can use yourself, creating a surplus.

The extra shoes are, in themselves, of little value to you. What you need is food, and you cannot achieve a well-balanced diet by consuming shoe leather and laces.

The farmer next door grows more food than he can consume himself. He too has a surplus of his product which will rot and be wasted if he cannot exchange it for something he wants.

In the meantime, the farmer does not enjoy plowing his fields in his bare feet. His field is invaded by sharp stones, prickly briars, ants that bite and bees that sting. He begins to look at your extra pile of shoes with a gleam in his eye.

He notices your shrinking waistline and grimacing face as you take another bite of a workboot. The farmer goes to his food locker and chooses a bushel of choice corn and plucks a couple of prime steaks from his freezer. He calls on you and plays "Let's make a deal."

"I will give you this food in exchange for a pair of workshoes," he offers.

You eagerly accept the terms of the transaction.

Who wins?

The purpose of trade and commerce is that both should win. Both should profit from the exchange.

The Impact of Scarcity and Surplus

The value of goods is determined by scarcity and surplus. Each wants what he does not have but what the other possesses. What is going on is not a sinful matter of coveting, but a human matter of community.

There is no such thing as a self-sufficient person. We are all dependent on the skill and labor of others to produce those things we cannot produce ourselves. What we do produce ourselves becomes valuable as a means of exchange with others.

When the exchange takes place freely, without a gun at the head, both sides profit. Each person gives up something he values less for something he values more. This is what profit is all about.

The Benefits of Competition

Who decides the value of the product? Only one person can determine the real value of a product for you, and that is you. The customer determines the price tag.

But, you protest, you did not choose to set the current price of gasoline; you did not choose to escalate the cost of building a home. The giant oil companies gain obscene profits by setting gas prices, and the building contractors and real estate salesmen jack up the price of houses to satisfy their own greed. They fix the prices, you argue, angry about rising costs.

Perhaps they do "fix the prices"—if they are stupid and are in a hurry to go out of business. Where trade is open to competition the customer benefits.

If someone charges too much for his goods, the people will refuse to buy them. The owner will then be left either with a rotting surplus to dispose of, a bankruptcy action to file or a decision to lower his prices to what the customer is willing to pay. People will not freely pay more for something than it is worth to them.

A man said to me through gritted teeth in 1978, "I will never pay a dollar a gallon for gasoline." So far he has not traded in his car for a bicycle. If he has kept his vow, I wonder where or how he is getting his gasoline.

The Law of Supply and Demand

In one sense, the most "free" economy is the black market. In the black market, scarce goods are exchanged for seemingly exorbitant prices. Why? Because people want to buy them and are willing to pay the price.

Ticket-scalping is illegal. The law prohibits selling tickets for sporting events above the price marked on the ticket. Yet scalping goes on because some people are willing to pay as much as $2,000 for a seat at the Super Bowl. That is the law of supply and demand at work.

The Importance of Productivity

We become most outraged about prices in times of famine and scarcity. Certain things are necessary for survival. Water is priceless to a man dying of thirst in the desert. So we sense the intolerable wickedness of the exploiter who comes by with a canteen of cool water, demanding an IOU for $100,000 per sip. And we despise the oppressor who takes advantage of a starving man's plight by demanding a million dollars for a loaf of bread.

Under normal circumstances water is plentiful, provided for us free from the heavens. Few get rich by exploiting its scarcity. The cost of food varies with the flux of famine and the

---

The desire of the working man is not elimination of profit but participation in it....To be a part owner in the operation enhances one's pride in his work.

---

bumper crop. That fact is why productivity is so vital to the well-being of mankind: *The more production, the less scarcity; the less the scarcity, the lower the cost; the lower the cost, the more people can enjoy the goods and services available to them.*

The Inevitability of Change

Prices change because the value of products changes for us. I am more willing to pay $3.00 for a hamburger when I am hungry than when I am full. I will not pay for something I do not want unless I am forced to do so.

Industry has changed dramatically in my lifetime. Consider the changes beyond that, extending to the last century and a quarter. In 1860, the leading industry in the northeastern United States was the whaling industry.

Why? Oil from the whale was a major commodity because it was used to illumine the American home at night. The oil lamp was a vast improvement over candlelight, making life at nighttime far more pleasant.

Where is the whaling industry now? What happened? A man

named Drake dug a hole in Titusville, Pennsylvania[14] and put the whalers out of business.

For about 10 years, the oil industry was riding high, as the principal use of oil was to make kerosene to illumine homes. Then the oil industry was threatened by Thomas Edison[15] who suddenly made the price of kerosene quite cheap. But oil made a comeback with the invention of the combustion engine and the appearance of the automobile.

Profit is tied to the relative value of goods and services and is essential to the survival of mankind. Business may be the occasion for evil—by cheating, false weights and measures, oppressive tactics—but it is not an intrinsic evil, nor even a "necessary evil." In itself, it is a good designed for the benefit of mankind whose dignity and worth include the body as well as the soul.

The Pride of Ownership

The desire of the working man is not elimination of profit but participation in it. Recent experiments in employee profit-sharing plans have encouraged the American labor force. To be a part owner in the operation enhances one's pride in his work.

The difference between laboring as a servant and laboring as an owner is illustrated by Jesus' image of the Good Shepherd. A contrast is seen between the shepherd who cares for his own sheep and the shepherd who is a "hireling." The owner goes the extra mile to protect the well-being of his property.

The property-sharing experiment gives workers a special interest in the product they are turning out. In a sense, their own names are attached to it. And when a product bears our name, our personal pride and self-esteem go wherever it goes.

I recently encountered a man who is the owner of a large manufacturing company in the Midwest. His products are shipped across the nation by trucks bearing the name of his company on the side panels. He was upset when he received a telephone call from an irate woman, calling to complain that she was the target of an obscene gesture made by one of the firm's truck drivers. She had noted the license number of the truck and was reporting the incident personally to the owner of the company. The man apologized profusely and promised that disciplinary action would be taken.

Checking the files, the owner was able to identify the driver and called him into his office. He said to the driver, "Do you realize that my name is printed on the side of your truck?"

The driver was duly contrite for his action and stood awaiting words of his dismissal. The owner did not fire the trucker, but exacted a more fitting punishment. He ordered his driver to return to the state where the incident occurred and to go personally to the home of the offended woman to offer his apology face-to-face.

Imagine the shock of the woman when she answered the doorbell to find an apologetic truck driver who had just driven several hundred miles to tell her he was sorry. One might suspect the trucker to be furious for the required mission; instead, he spoke of gaining a new respect for his company and its policies. In acting to redress the insult to the woman, he experienced an increase in his own self-esteem.

He also got a taste of the pride that goes with ownership.

REFORMATION OR REVOLUTION?

One benefit of the economic crisis that has plagued the automobile industry is that labor and management have been forced to take new steps in mutual cooperation. Labor, for example, has willingly given up hard-won benefits to reduce the market price of cars and to restore a competitive base to the company. The vested interests of both labor and management have a point of meeting on common ground. All concerned understand that no one profits when a company folds.

Estrangement Still Exists

The fact remains, however, that estrangement still exists between labor and management. The roots of the hostility run deep and cannot be expected to be healed by superficial measures. An odd factor persists in the work place: while contract disputes continue to focus heavily on economic issues, the individual complaints of the worker tend to be of a noneconomic sort.

Human Dignity Must Be Recognized

In candid interviews with scores of laborers, I find the accent not on compensation so much as on the recognition of their human dignity. Of course, that accent is different as one moves from union to union or job situation to job situation. In newly organized fields where little financial gain has been achieved, the economic accent is greater. But in a labor environment where the union is well-established and years have been spent negotiating strong contracts, little complaint is heard about financial compensation. The focus there is on working conditions and morale problems.

What comes out of these discussions is a heightened awareness of the importance of worker morale. I have heard workers articulate that their concern at the bargaining table is not economic justice, but revenge for personal slights suffered at the hands of unscrupulous supervisors. The bargaining table is the place where the aggrieved can get even.

Since dignity is so difficult to measure in quantitative terms, revenge is often translated into dollars and cents. The insult to dignity is then redressed by a pay raise. The pay scale becomes the measuring rod for one's value.

Reformation Is Not Easily Achieved

The Christian concerned for reformation in the work world feels the weight of Marx's complaints. He is aware that there is some truth to the charge that religion can be used as a tool to exploit the worker. The American worker jealously guards his freedom of religion. Few things are more repugnant to him than having religion forced down his throat.

Reformation is not achieved easily and is far more difficult to implement than a bloody revolution. The revolution promises swift and dramatic change, but all too often it results in the babies being thrown out with the bathwater.

Economic Change Must Come

When people are displeased with the status quo, something has to give. Change must come, either in orderly fashion or violently. Angry people tend to be impatient with the former and grasp for the latter when the opportunity is presented. It is urgent that significant changes come to the work world, and they can come about peaceably through negotiation and compromise, if there is requisite goodwill and just intentions on all sides. Now is the time for us all "to do justly, and to love mercy" (Mic. 6:8, *KJV*).

Marxism Still Holds Appeal

Marxism is presently in retreat in many places in the world and various forms of democratic government are rising in its place. Though Marxism is wounded and fallen, it is not yet dead. It still holds a tattered appeal to some, and a remnant of hard-liners still carry its banner.

So we must remember that capitalism has yet to win as many converts as has democracy. How tragic it would be to see the supreme model of economic freedom become another statistic, replaced by another *ism*, whether Marxist or otherwise, yet just as revolutionary and doctrinaire, complete with its false economic ideologues, camouflaging their repressive aims with glowing promises of illusionary economic Utopias.

Transitions Are Difficult and Dangerous

Even now in eastern Europe, newly won political freedoms are in danger of being undermined by the economic chaos left in the wake of crumbling totalitarian rule. The leaders of the new governments in the USSR, Romania and elsewhere are finding that economic progress tends to lag behind political change. Already in the USSR as increased unrest and civil disturbances combine with unfulfilled expectations, warnings are being sounded that the country could once again slip back under dictatorial rule in an effort to reestablish law and order—even though there appears no possibility of a return to old-style Marxism.

Revolution Is Still Possible

Certainly, the future of Europe's former Iron Curtain countries is uncertain at best. And tragically, for the people in them, the woes of repressions newly shed start to dim and begin to appear almost preferable in the face of looming joblessness, poverty and hunger. During the instability of change and transition, voices begin to cry out that the old was better than the new, not unlike the Israelites of the Exodus, grumbling against Moses and Aaron and saying, "If only we had died by the Lord's hand in Egypt! There we sat around pots of meat and ate all the food we wanted, but you have brought us out into this desert to starve this entire assembly to death" (Exod. 16:3, *NIV*).

So the concluding words of the *Communist Manifesto* still have an ominous ring to them: "Let the ruling classes tremble at a communist revolution. The proletarians have nothing to lose but their chains. They have a world to win. WORKING MEN OF ALL COUNTRIES, UNITE!"

FOR FURTHER REFLECTION

1. What were your feelings about communism during the McCarthy era?
2. What do you think about creating a synthesis between Marxism and Christianity?
3. How important are economic clashes to the development of history?
4. Do you think a wage earner is an economic slave? Why or why not?
5. What is the difference between economic equality and economic equity?
6. List ways that tools affect production where you work.
7. Is profit an evil?
8. Does our legal system reflect legislation favoring special interest groups? If so, what problems does this create?
9. What does the phrase "you cannot legislate morality" mean? List laws that do not touch moral questions.
10. How are economic freedom and political freedom related?

CHAPTER TEN

DIGNITY IN THE WORKPLACE

WAYNE Alderson was jarred to attention by the strident ringing of the telephone, an annoying intrusion into a frenetic schedule that was turning him into an adrenalin addict. The reverie interrupted was one of self-pity, the type men have on the rim of burnout. Alderson was tired, and with the fatigue came a disconsolate spirit that prodded his brain with thoughts of quitting the crusade.

The Crusade
Alderson's crusade for a new style of labor-management relations under the banner of the Value of the Person had catapulted him into a role of national leadership. His ideas were penetrating organized labor and the White House, and were being carried across the sea to Poland.

Only hours before being taken into custody and placed under house arrest in December 1981, Lech Walesa was seen gesticulating wildly, brandishing a copy of *Stronger Than Steel*, the story of Wayne Alderson's life and struggle for human dignity.

The book was a legacy from Lech's father, whose body had been flown from the United States to be interred in Polish soil. The casket conveying the senior Walesa included a few artifacts from his life in America, including a copy of the book that provoked renewed hope in his final months.

A crusade can be adventuresome, even glamorous for a while. Much adulation had come Wayne's way with all the external signs of success. Television talk shows, prestigious conference events, and even a movement by some prominent business leaders to have Alderson appointed to the president's cabinet as secretary of labor had done much at the time to buoy his spirits.

The Depression
But when the enemy does not surrender easily and the grail remains captive, the mission turns to mocking drudgery. Alderson was now braving his own kind of house arrest, a bondage of the soul bogged down by bouts of depression. He did not dream about a work-world reformation; the dream had long before been forged into a practical goal. When the dream was transformed into a goal, thought turned to action and action into reaction.

Most of the reaction had been positive and enthusiastic; but not all. Resistance to change can be mighty, especially when one is meddling with the power structures of business and industry and tampering with long-established policies.

So the concrete realities of change in the workplace came at a snail's pace. And Alderson desperately wanted to get beyond the hoopla to real reform.

The Phone Call
The phone refused to cease its jangling, so Wayne moved to answer it.

The voice on the other end was weak, evidencing clear signs of distress. "It's Shelby, Mr. Wayne.... He's real, real sick."

"Where is he?" Wayne whispered into the phone as he felt his own spirit sink more deeply.

His stomach sickened as the import of the call stabbed him. He got the name of the hospital and promised the frightened woman that he would come at once.

Nancy Alderson read the look on her husband's face as he cradled the phone, and knew the news was grim. "It's Shelby, hon, he's dying. I have to go."

Protests about a ruined dinner were improper, and Nancy's compassion for Shelby united her own spirit to Wayne's, making all domestic routines inconsequential at the moment. The loss of normalcy in the Alderson household was still a nagging ache, but Nancy had made her peace with it years before. She was now a veteran of the crisis of the urgent and handled it with equanimity.

The Visit

Wayne entered the ward where the critically ill were housed, and he saw Shelby before Shelby saw him. The gaunt, emaciated frame of a man before him was obviously beyond medical hope. As Wayne approached the bed, a glint of recognition flashed in Shelby's eyes, and a smile made with effort spread across his black face.

Shelby rasped, "I know'd you'd come, Mr. Wayne, I just know'd it."

Wayne took his aged friend's hand and thought about how Shelby always called him "Mr. Wayne." He found the deferential name embarrassing, as it communicated a former era of paternalism—a bygone age when the "darkie" slave called his plantation master by his first name and prefaced it with the social courtesy of "mister."

Wayne understood that such expressions were anathema to post-civil rights movement African-Americans. And some in these generations would say that Shelby Rowe—genuinely courteous to everyone, black or white—was an "Uncle Tom" who had never made the transition. Anger boiled in Wayne's gut at the thought that anyone at all would consider Shelby an Uncle Tom, simply because he still spoke in a manner that had long since become second nature for him.

Wayne looked down at his old friend and told himself, *"Nobody can work for 35 years in the grueling role of a chipper in a steel foundry and be considered a 'boy.' So never mind Shelby's antiquated speech patterns,"* he mused. *"This is a man."*

Wayne could still envision the image of Shelby standing with his chipper's gun attacking a giant mold. His wiry build seemed a fluid flow of muscles as the sweat glistened from his ebony arms. But that was yesterday, and the years of toil and the ravages of disease had dismissed the muscle and replaced it with sagging flesh on a shrunken frame.

Shelby knew how to work—entering the mills as a young lad, transplanted from his boyhood home in Georgia. His parents had fled the South following the "drinking gourd" that led their ancestors to freedom.

Shelby's paternal grandfather had been a slave, and his father was the first in the family to make the transition to liberty. And Shelby, in turn, was one of the first to "enlist" in the Value of the Person movement that brought a dramatic turnaround in the foundry where he labored under Alderson's leadership.

For Shelby, the war against prejudice and labor-management antagonism was now coming to an end. He would not live to see the victory of human dignity in the workplace.

In his lifetime, Shelby had witnessed some great gains for black people in America: the desegregation of the armed forces by President Harry S Truman; the outlawing by the U.S. Supreme Court in 1954 of all segregated public education; the victory of the Reverend Martin Luther King, Jr. when his 1955-56 Montgomery, Alabama bus boycott ended with the Supreme Court banning all segregated public transportation in the city; and the advent of fair housing and hiring practices.

The Promise

But Shelby's dream went beyond concerns that were purely racial or ethnic. He also wanted to see a work environment where all people were treated with dignity.

To speak was difficult for Shelby, but he strained to find words of consolation and encouragement for Wayne. Alderson had come to this place to bring comfort but found himself being consoled instead.

Somehow, it seemed as if Shelby could see right through Wayne and read his secret thoughts. For seeing Shelby like this was pushing Wayne to the border of despair, making him think, "If this is all there is—why bother?"

But Shelby did not accept defeat, and he refused to allow Alderson to accept it either. "Whatever happens, Mr. Wayne, don't quit. You just gotta keep going."

Wayne squeezed Shelby's hand and said, "I won't quit, Shelby. I promise."

Shelby nodded his head and relaxed his grip on Wayne's hand. The oath had been uttered, and it was enough. "OK, Mr. Wayne, OK. It's OK."

So-called sophisticates recoil at melodrama and dismiss such deathbed pacts as too maudlin to be taken seriously. Wayne Alderson's humanity, however, overshadows any such pseudosophistication. Shelby grasped that fact and knew he was not listening to "honky jive."

The Resolve

He had learned to trust Alderson's word. Alderson was capable of voluminous profanity, but he never profaned a promise to his men. He had proven it in a spider trench in the Siegfried Line[1] and had been demonstrating it ever since in the steel mills and coal mines of another battlefield.

Wayne whispered, "I love you, Shelby," as he leaned over and kissed his friend good-bye.

In only a matter of hours, Shelby Rowe entered the final rest of a workingman. He died in transcendent peace. For Alderson, it was settled as well; he would entertain no more thoughts of quitting.

The Question

Still, Shelby Rowe's dying passion snaps our attention to the question: Why did it mean so much to this mortally ill African-American laborer that Wayne Alderson not quit?

In simple terms, what Wayne Alderson meant to Shelby Rowe was that Rowe's long years of backbreaking labor were not futile. The thought that such effort was meaningless was repugnant to his soul.

In that respect, Shelby Rowe was not unique; every human being, from the lowest-paid unskilled laborer to the most highly-positioned corporate executive, wants to know that his labor has real value.

To know your labor counts is to be assured that you count.

THE VALUE OF THE PERSON MOVEMENT

The Movement

Alderson did not quit. He has continued, relentlessly pursuing a work-world reformation built upon a concept of management called The Value of the Person. The Value of the Person movement is gaining momentum as it spreads to industries and businesses across the nation.

The movement sometimes appears under a different guise, but the concept is the same. Elements of it are found in various experimental methods of management such as those contained in Quality Circle, Participative Management and Performance Management. It was Lech Walesa's father who declared, "The Solidarity movement in Poland is the Value of the Person movement."

The Moment

Alderson has taken his concept to every state in the continental United States in the past decade and a half. His most poignant moment in these years has not come in the White House or the Parliament Building of Canada, but in a spot a thousand feet beneath the surface of the earth.

Wayne journeyed to Benton, Illinois, to visit with personnel of the Inland Coal Company. A meeting was arranged with the miners in the belly of the mine itself. As he stepped into the entrance of the shaft to be carried to the millenarian depth, Wayne noticed the modernized equipment that gave a face-lift to the operation.

He joined 65 miners cramped into an elevator to descend to the floor below. Machines present in the two-mile corridor beneath the ground were in stark contrast to the primitive implements Wayne remembered from the days of his youth.

Forty years had passed since Alderson had stepped into a coal mine. To the Christian, the span of four decades has almost a mystical ring to it. Moses spent 40 years in solitude in the Midianite desert (Acts 7:29-30). The Israelites wandered 40 years in the wilderness (Num. 14:33).

Forty days and nights of rain brought the deluge (Gen. 7:4) which spared only Noah and his family. For 40 days, Christ endured the assault of Satan (Luke 4:2). The number 40 has no magical cabalism to it, but the fact of it made Alderson feel eerie.

The Mines

The interior of a coal mine has changed from the early days of

John L. Lewis (1880-1969) and the rampages of the "iron and coal police." The company store has vanished and the kerosene-illumined headlamp has gone the way of the horse and buggy. And no longer do mule-drawn carts tug their loads through the labyrinth of tunnels.

Some things, however, remain the same. The dank walls of the mine still give rise to the sickening feeling of claustrophobia, and no modern machine has been invented to sweep the mine floor clean of its layers of coal dust. The specter of death hangs always in the air, as the cave-in has not been eliminated from the miner's perilous task.

Most of all, the people remain the same, save for the new presence of women in the mines. The same look Wayne remembered on the faces of the miners he grew up with was registered in the eyes of the miners of Benton. The same lines of weariness were etched on their faces as they huddled in the soot-filled shaft to talk with Wayne.

Alderson looked down and, in the shadows, his eyes fixed on the imprint of a miner's boot in the coal dust. The image of each line of the tread was delicately raised in the powder, like the symmetrical latticework of a spider's web. The sight of the footprint snapped Wayne into a time-warp of memory, back to his childhood when his father and grandfather took him into the mines of Canonsburg, Pennsylvania to play "miner."

As a boy he was allowed to help his father by picking up loose bits of coal and placing them in the mule cart. He always walked behind his father, shielded by him in the event of a dreaded slate fall. He remembered vividly the ritual he made of placing his small feet precisely in the center of the footprints his father's boots left in the dust in front of him.

The Message

Now, as he gazed at the footprint of the modern miner, Wayne thought of the steps he had taken in the past 40 years. He smiled to himself as he thought of the news which had just reached him from his boyhood home of Canonsburg. The message reported that B.C. Coleman, the president of the local union of the United Steel Workers (USW), had just succeeded in getting the Value of the Person explicitly written into a contract agreement with McGraw Edison.

The news was particularly significant as McGraw Edison was

The worker...wants to be noticed, to be deemed valuable, not to be embraced as the bosom buddy of the boss.

---

the largest industry in Canonsburg, with a work force of 4,000 employees. And numbered in that multitude were Wayne's brother, his cousin and a host of boyhood chums. As Wayne enjoyed this moment of reverie, he recalled the homespun precept his father and mother never tired of telling him, "Son, never forget where you came from."

The Memories

Alderson remembers. He remembers well his roots in poverty and humiliation. He remembers his days as a soldier, standing "on the point" for his infantry unit in World War II. He remembers the grenade in a spider trench of the Siegfried Line which exploded in his face.

He remembers the heroic sacrifice of Charles "Red" Preston who was killed while shielding Alderson from further injury. He remembers the years of surgery and recuperation, his marriage to Nancy Holt and his trek to night school to earn a college degree. He remembers his rise in the corporate structures to the rank of vice president of operations of a large steel foundry.

The Maverick

And he remembers being a maverick manager who broke the unwritten rules of management.

CROSSING THE LINE

Though some will howl in protest to the contrary, the work world gives strong evidence of a firm though unspoken rule: *management may not walk with labor.* Such rules are not found in printed policy manuals of the company, yet they exist and are often enforced with iron discipline. In former days, unwritten rules of hiring Irish Catholics or Jews were likewise enforced, but are generally disappearing from the prejudice of management.

The rule of nonassociation with labor still holds firm, and for a manager to break it with impunity is difficult. However, the rule must be thrown in the ashcan if there is to be any hope of labor-management reconciliation. Segregation breeds discrimination like swamps nurture mosquitoes.

Breaking the Rule

To break this rule requires a heavy dose of moral courage. It takes someone secure enough to do what is right, regardless of the disapproval of his peers.

It is Jesus eating with tax collectors (Mark 2:15) and drinking from the same well as a Samaritan harlot (John 4:4-30). It is Stonewall Jackson sharing a canteen with a buck private. It is Mother Teresa touching the pariahs of Calcutta. It is "Doc" living in John Steinbeck's *Cannery Row*. It is Wayne Alderson walking through a foundry wearing a safety helmet painted black.

When the rule is violated, people notice it. The oppressed are heartened and the powerful are incensed.

Walking with Labor

Association, Not Imitation. For the Value of the Person to succeed, it is not necessary to eliminate the executives' privileges which give honor to their high office. Workers do not despise the prerogatives of management, but they loathe being ignored. Sociological studies reveal that workers do not want their managers to dress like them or to abandon the accoutrements of rank. In fact, the workers often take vicarious pride in the status of their leaders.

The Englishman is honored when the Queen stops and talks with him but he does not want Her Majesty to adopt the dress style of the cockney barmaid. Egalitarian sameness, as seen in the dress style of communist China, is oppressive to the human spirit. Rank and its forms may distinguish us, but they ought not to divide us into the categories of the valuable and the valueless.

Recognition, Not Renunciation. The great fear of management is that walking with labor will somehow demean the status they have worked so hard to achieve. Managers also desire recognition and cling tenaciously to the privileges of their position.

The irony is that when managers come off their pedestals of power to mingle with the grassroots employees, their dignity is not demeaned but enhanced. Wayne Alderson walked with labor, but he still wore his white shirt and his Christian Dior ties. In fact, because he remained every ounce the manager, his concern for the worker was so appreciated.

Equity, Not Equality. Though workers demand equal pay for equal tasks, they do not expect to be paid salaries equal to those of management. Again, the difference is between equality and equity. Equity calls for justice, not a communal plan of equalized pay. More skillful work is more valuable to the operation and is worthy of more pay.

Esteem, Not Embrace. Walking with labor does not mean

total fraternization. The worker neither expects nor desires that the president of the company spend his social time with him. That only makes for social discomfort. What he wants is to be noticed, to be deemed valuable, not to be embraced as the bosom buddy of the boss.

WORKER RECOGNITION

Every worker has a name. His name is his most jealously guarded possession, as it identifies the essence of his person.

When people I admire greet me by name, my spirit soars; when they look at me without recognition, my spirit sinks. When my name is mispronounced—especially when it is made to sound like "growl"—my ears recoil as when someone scrapes his fingernails across a chalkboard. My spinal cord records the annoyance as the fibers of my nervous system register the irritation.

Know Names and Faces
The worker hurts when a manager addresses him, "Hey you." Each person wants to be known by name, not by an impersonal number or by a demeaning racial or ethnic slur. Nicknames are fine as long as they accent a positive character trait. Let the sobriquet call attention to a weakness or physical blemish, like "motor-mouth" for the one who stutters, "bucky" for the one with protruding teeth, and the name becomes a hammer blow of indignity.

Every manager at some time in his life has been required to practice the discipline of rote memorization. Perhaps it was with multiplication tables, chemistry symbols or the tense endings of Latin verbs. How much easier it is to spend the short time required to memorize the names and faces of the people working around you every day. It can be done even if the work force numbers in the hundreds.

Value the Person

To be a manager has some parallels with the job description of the mechanic. The mechanic's job is to insure that the equipment and machinery of the operation are well-maintained and repaired in the event of a breakdown. Similarly and more importantly, a manager's job is to be concerned for the well-being of his workers.

A person suffering from illness or grief is not a very productive worker. To minister to the well-being of the worker is far more important than the maintenance of a machine. Consequently, one of Wayne Alderson's favorite aphorisms is, "The value of people has to come before the value of the machine."

Keep in Touch

Being in touch with people in times of difficulty gives management leaders a fresh understanding of their work force. I listened recently as the president and chairman of the board of a Fortune 500 corporation told of his conversion to the Value of the Person program.

As the chief executive of a corporation closely linked to the basic steel industry, he had had a prior mild interest in the Value of the Person. His involvement in it, however, was sparse and somewhat token. His conversion to "true believer" took place almost fortuitously.

During the months when steel mills in and around Pittsburgh were closing like windows in a rainstorm, the executive was enjoying a Saturday morning working in his garden. Abandoned by his wife for a shopping spree, the man was left to fend for himself at lunchtime. While still garbed in grubby overalls, he jumped in his car and went to a local tavern for lunch.

The tavern was a favorite haunt of mill workers from a plant which, just days before, had shut its doors. They were congregated around the bar, drowning their sorrows in the local mixture of whiskey and beer known by various names, such as "a shot and a beer," "a boilermaker" or, most expressively, "a rooter and a hooter."

The executive slipped incognito into a corner space and listened attentively to the dreary tales of men freshly unemployed. With no way to insulate himself from their talk, he listened to their uninhibited conversation. His presence was not noted, as he was mysterious to them, a modern version of Mark Twain's *Mysterious Stranger.*

The conversation the executive overheard struck a profound chord in him and left him inwardly "radicalized." He commanded the destiny of people like that every day and discovered he had been out of touch with their human needs. His "visit" was accidental, but it provided a taste of what can be learned when management takes the time to go out of their way to hear the cries of their people.

Communicate Positive Attitudes

Attitudes are what create the mood of a working environment. And attitudes, both positive and negative, are communicated with words and by actions.

Keep Verbal Communication Respectful. It is important that the words and the tone of language used in office and industry communication be respectful. Strident, harsh or forceful language antagonizes people.

I remember one executive officer who was enthused after a seminar and determined to implement the Value of the Person in his factory. His first action was to draft a memo to his management team announcing the beginning of the program.

The memo was terse, "You are mandated to attend a meeting to discuss plans for implementing the Value of the Person." I chuckled at the presence of the word *mandated* in the memo. Rather than calling attention to this violation of the spirit of the program directly, I took the indirect route of playing Nathan to his David (see 2 Sam. 12:1-15).

I related an experience I had as a young college professor when I found a memo in my faculty mailbox with the words, "Professor Sproul—you are required to come to the dean's office immediately." My blood was boiling as I made my way across the quadrangle to the administration building.

A person who has responsibility for a task must also have the authority that is commensurate with that responsibility.

When I approached the desk in the office, I smiled pleasantly and asked, "Who sent me this memo?"

One of the senior secretaries responded by saying that she had drafted the memo.

Calmly and politely, I said, "Miss, I want to tell you the story of something that happened to me when I was a little boy. I used to play in my backyard with my friend Donny. Donny and I loved to play cars in my sandbox as it was just after the war and metal cars were a novelty that delighted us."

As I was telling the story, the woman looked at me as if I were crazy, wondering why in the world I was telling her these things. But I continued the narrative.

"One day as dinner time approached, and Donny and I were absorbed with our sandbox game, my mother poked her head out of the window and called, 'Son, it's time to come in for dinner.'

"I responded like Henry Aldrich, old-time radio's ageless teen, 'Coming, Mother.'

"Only I didn't go into the house. I was having so much fun

in the sand, I wanted to squeeze every playful moment out of it. I quickly forgot my mother's summons until she appeared in front of me scowling, with her hands on her hips.

"She said in authoritarian tones, 'Young man, you get in this house *immediately!*"

At that point in the narrative, my countenance abruptly changed and my voice took on a deadly tone as I said to the secretary, "Miss _____, that happened when I was six years old. Since then no one has ever told me to do anything 'immediately,' and don't think you can start now."

I threw the memo on the desk in front of her and walked out. She got the message.

I did not need to recite Nathan's punchline, "Thou art the man" (2 Sam. 12:7, *KJV*) to the amused plant manager. He too got the message and changed the wording of his memo. He realized that language and word usage communicate attitudes.

Understand Nonverbal Communication. Communication on the job goes far beyond verbal communication. The subtleties of nonverbal communication are read closely, especially by those who are streetwise.

The analysis of *body language* and other forms of nonverbal communication is a recently developing science. Studies are made of the tilt of the chin, the posture of men at a bargaining table, the rapid eye movements of sleep patterns and the degree of pupil dilation that takes place in flirting. Police interrogators and practicing psychiatrists must become masters of the art of interpreting such body language.

A *hidden language* is also found in wearing apparel, home decorations and office furnishings. Few secret hiding places are left where we can retreat from the analysis of others.

If one's desk is too big, it reveals his insecurity; elevated on a dais, it exposes his megalomania. If he stays behind it while talking to subordinates, it sends *one kind of signal,* and if he comes from behind it to greet them, *another set of signals* is transmitted.

If a man's home is his castle, then his office is his fortress. An awareness of this truth tells us that we also need to be aware of another important facet of nonverbal communication: the *significance of the meetingplace.*

Where we choose to encounter our fellow workers is important to worker morale. Being summoned to the manager's office recalls, for many, the leaded weight in the pit of the stomach that appeared instantly with the teacher's words, "Go to the principal's office."

To choose instead to go and visit a person on his own turf is to acknowledge his status as an individual. As one executive said, "Each man is a king in his own house. Why should we treat him like a pauper here?"

Create the Right Mood

Trying to keep track of all these unspoken forms of communication admittedly can give a manager an Excedrin headache or unleash the demons of paranoia. Nevertheless, what we said earlier bears repeating:

Attitudes are what create the mood of a working environment. And attitudes, both positive and negative, are communicated with words *and* by actions.

POWER AND AUTHORITY

Understanding the Difference

Managers need to understand the difference between power and authority. People with authority have power, while not all people with power have authority. The chairman of the board has both.

Authority has to do with the *right* to command or impose obligation. Power has to do with the *ability to enforce* the command. The policeman's badge represents his authority while his stick represents his power, a power which can easily degenerate into intimidation.

The pastor in the local church knows the difference between power and authority. The elder or vestryman has authority. He sits on the governing boards of the church and casts the weight of his vote in the decision-making process.

The church's largest donor may hold no office of authority but yields enormous power by the threat of withdrawing his financial support. Many a session's decisions have been influenced or even overturned by the unauthorized power-broker in the church.

Responsibility Without Authority

The structures of management must be established to insure an equity of authority and responsibility. A person who has responsibility for a task must also have the authority that is commensurate with that responsibility.

To assign responsibility without the corresponding authority is to doom the employee to failure through no fault of his own. If the needed authority is lacking, the employee may seek to substitute unauthorized power tactics to meet his responsibilities. Here the fuzzy organizational chart of the muddled job description may be the breeding ground for tyranny.

The Supreme Example

The supreme example of the conjunction of power and authority is found in God Himself. His power is omnipotent and His authority is sovereign.

The maxim, "Power tends to corrupt and absolute power corrupts absolutely,"[2] may apply to men but not to the Deity, for added to the attributes of God are holiness and grace. No mortal will ever convict God of a misuse of power or an abuse of authority, as His rule is righteous with no shadow of turning in it.

God's power is tempered by grace and His authority by compassion. He is slow to anger and patient with rebellious and slothful subordinates. His judgments are fair and His gifts to men generous. His ways are not the ways of the celestial tyrant or the cosmic bully.

The same may be said of Christ to whom was given "all authority in heaven and on earth" (Matt. 28:18, *RSV*). Both the Father and the Son exhibit the delicate balance of power and grace. In that example is a lesson worthy of the attention of every person in authority.

Tempering with Grace

The more authority one has, the easier it is to be gracious. The more power one has, the easier it is to be kind. God is secure in His power, as it is absolute and immutable.

We humans lack those guarantees of future security, making for the insecure tactics of tyranny lest we lose the power we have. The secure leader walks softly when carrying the big stick.[3] The bully walks loudly, to conceal the little stick he bears.

The bottom line of power is that the more you have, the more you need to temper it with grace, and the easier it is to do so.

Oppression Through Policy

Oppression comes to a work force not only from the intimidating tactics of the individual abuse of power, but from ill-conceived policy manuals as well. I have twice witnessed spontaneous revolts of staffs to the presentation of policy manuals—once in a seminary faculty meeting, and the second in a staff meeting of my present organization. In both cases, a wildcat walkout was threatened as people reacted furiously to being treated as children.

Why do such reactions occur? Why does the unrest explode over a company's rigid policies?

One crucial factor in the policy debate is the making of a general policy to restrain a small percentage of irresponsible workers. Examine the policy of your company.

For whom are the policies written? Are they demeaning and insulting to mature adults? Are the policies spelled out really necessary? Are the rules aimed at the 5 percent of the work force who are troublemakers or at the 95 percent who are not?

Morale of the full work force would be better served by eliminating the 5 percent who are irresponsible and writing the policy manual for the rest. Or if termination is made impossible by union protection rules, deal with the 5 percent separately.

Most operations are overpoliced. A more effective approach is to keep the policies to a minimum and enforce the ones you have.

A fair policy code need not compromise company standards of excellence. Strictness in quality control is not tyranny.

The Worker/Home Relationship

We must be keenly aware of the intimate relationship that exists between a worker and his home. No one leaves his work at the office. By including family members in the life of the foundry through scheduled "family-day picnics," the employees were made more aware of the personal character of their colaborers' lives, and the workers' families gained a higher appreciation for what their breadwinners were doing during their working hours.

I witnessed a factory owner of a midwestern mill dismiss a man from his post for that day for an unusual reason. The owner of the mills was aware that the man's son was playing in a championship baseball game that afternoon and insisted that the working father leave his post to attend the game. The owner said, "Your son needs you today more than I do."

I discovered that this owner's normal practice was to grant

time off with full pay to workers whose children were involved in events special to them. The owner wanted his workers to be good parents as well as productive employees. His policy of family concern cannot be measured on the balance sheet by the most astute of cost accountants, but if worker turnover rate has anything to do with overhead costs, that man's policy is as profitable as it is humane.

Cultivating Human Dignity

Where human dignity is cultivated in a work environment, increased production and higher quality are its inevitable by-products. America's workers are still her most important natural resource. No machine has yet been invented that can dispense with the need for people.

The poorest laborer has more dignity in his fingernail than a computer has in its total complex circuitry. The machine has its intricate mechanisms and delicate parts, but like the scarecrow in the land of Oz, it has no heart.

Machines do not picket their places of employment. Type-writers and intercoms never demand a raise. Machine presses never engage in collective bargaining. Copy machines do not indulge in office politics. The machine has no aching void because it cannot feel pain.

But the worker has a heart, and it breaks within him when he is treated without dignity. When his dignity is honored and the void is filled, then the sanctity of labor—his labor—is affirmed.

FOR FURTHER REFLECTION

1. What role does God have in the work place?
2. Does your place of work have unwritten rules? What are they?

3. What are the major noneconomic issues which provoke strikes?
4. How would you describe the difference between power and authority?
5. Is there an adversary style of labor and management in your community? Where?
6. List ways worker morale and dignity can be improved.
7. How does the atmosphere of the work place affect your home?
8. What would it take to have a work-world reformation?
9. How important is human dignity to productivity?
10. Have you seen the documentary film *Miracle of Pittron?*[4] What were your impressions?

Notes

Chapter 1

1. Charles McCarry, *Double Eagle* (Boston: Little, Brown and Company, 1979).
2. The anonymous saying, "Winning isn't everything, it's the only thing," is often attributed to the late coach Vince Lombardi. But what he actually said in a 1962 interview is "Winning isn't everything, but wanting to win is."
3. Pat Conroy, *The Lords of Discipline* (New York: Bantam Books, 1982), p. 266.

Chapter 2

1. The actual wording of Aristotle's quotation from his *Metaphysics*, book I, chapter 1, reads, "It is of itself that the divine thought thinks (since it is the most excellent of things), and its thinking is a thinking on thinking."
2. William Shakespeare, *The Merchant of Venice*, IV, i, 184.
3. Jonathan Edwards, *Charity and Its Fruits* (Carlisle, PA: Banner of Truth Trust, published 1852, reprinted 1978), p. 23.
4. The "Elephant Man" was Joseph "John" Merrick of England, born in 1862. Because of a horribly disfiguring disease that caused him to grow a large protuberance on his face, he spent most of his short life on exhibit as a professional freak. Rescued and befriended by Sir Frederick Treves, surgeon to Queen Victoria and King Edward VII, Merrick was given shelter in the London Hospital. Here he lived for the last four years of his life, able at last to live decently and to achieve a measure of social acceptability. He died at London Hospital in his sleep in 1890 at the age of 28.
5. Early in 1892, in Homestead, Pennsylvania, the National Amalgamated Association of Iron and Steel Workers called a labor strike against the Homestead Steel Works, a division of the Carnegie Steel Company. The strike lasted 143 days and ended in a victory for the steel company.

   On July 6, 200 Pinkerton detectives, serving as company guards, opened fire on the striking pickets, causing a riot in which seven men were killed and 20 or more wounded. To restore order, the governor sent in the entire state militia, dispersing the striking workers who were then replaced by nonunion labor.

The Homestead Strike is remembered as one of the nation's most violent and bloody strikes and is believed to have retarded unionization of the steel industry until late in the 1930s.

6. In Greek mythology, Gordius was a peasant of Phrygia who used a cleverly tied knot to secure the yoke of his ox to the cart. Later, Gordius became Phrygia's king and dedicated his cart and yoke to Zeus (Jupiter). According to legend, whoever could undo the knot tied by Gordius would become the next ruler of Asia. Alexander the Great cut the knot with his sword and announced that he had fulfilled the prophecy.

Over time, "cutting the Gordian knot" has come to mean solving by unusual means a problem that is insoluble in its own terms.

Chapter 3

1. "What a chimera then is man! What a novelty! What a monster, what a chaos, what a contradiction, what a prodigy! Judge of all things, feeble earthworm, depository of truth, a sink of uncertainty and error, the glory and the shame of the universe." Blaise Pascal (1623-1662), *Pensées*, no. 434.

2. Seutonius, *Lives of the Caesars, Julius*, sec. 37. Spoken by Caesar in Greek, according to Seutonius. The translation in English: "You also, Brutus my son."

3. A reference to "A Boy Named 'Sue,'" a country and western song popularized by singer Johnny Cash.

4. *Macbeth*, V, v, 17.

5. The Age of Enlightenment was a philosophic movement of the eighteenth century that rejected traditional social, religious and political ideas and emphasized rationalism.

6. The Baron Paul Henri Dietrich d'Holbach (1723-1789) was one of Europe's prominent intellectual figures of the mid-1700s. Influential among French revolutionary thinkers he espoused a materialism which held that a kind of blind "necessity" rules the world.

7. These are the opening words of a sonnet, "The New Colossus," written in 1883 by Emma Lazarus (1849-1887) and inscribed on a tablet in the pedestal of the Statue of Liberty.

8. Variations of this phrase have been used as a synonym for World War I. "A war to end war" was one of the slogans popularized by a governmental Committee on Public Information set up during WWI to support and justify involvement by the U.S.A. in the war. And H. G. Wells in 1914 published a book with the title *The War That Will End War*. Bertrand Russell, in his *Portraits from Memory*, also attributes the phrase "a war to end war" to Wells.

9. Although combat in World War I ended at 11:00 A.M. on November 11,

1918 when Germany accepted the Armistice, the war did not officially end until the Treaty of Versailles was signed on June 28, 1919 in the Hall of Mirrors of the Palace of Versailles at Versailles, France.

10. In September 1938, Neville Chamberlain, then the British Prime Minister—in the hopes of appeasing Adolf Hitler and avoiding another world war—met with Hitler in Munich, Germany, and signed the Munich Pact. He then returned home to London and announced from 10 Downing Street that he had achieved "peace in our time." Nazi Germany's subsequent invasion of Poland quickly proved that Hitler had succeeded in tricking Chamberlain who was then forced to resign his office in May 1940. He was succeeded as Prime Minister by Sir Winston Churchill who guided Britain through the ensuing war years.

11. This German word originated in 1939 and translates literally as "lightning war."

12. The Roman orator Cicero is the source of the story of Damocles, a courtier in the service of Greek King Dionysius the Elder (431?-367 B.C.), a tyrant who once ruled the city-state of Syracuse. Damocles talked so much about the happy lot of kings that Dionysius decided to teach him a lesson.

    The king invited Damocles to a banquet and seated the courtier in his own place at the table. Damocles enjoyed the honor until he looked up and saw suspended over his head a sword hanging by a single hair.

    In this way, Dionysius sought to teach Damocles that even a king experiences uncertainty in life. Subsequently, the expression, "sword of Damocles," has come to mean a fearful or approaching circumstance that could occur at any time.

13. Harvard psychologist B(urrus) F(rederic) Skinner (1904-1990) was America's leading exponent of the behaviorist school of psychology which holds that human behavior is explained in terms of physiological responses to external stimuli. Among other things, Skinner advocated mass conditioning as a means of social control. One of his better known books is *Beyond Freedom and Dignity* (1971).

14. Dante Alighieri, *The Divine Comedy* [c. 1310-1320], *Inferno*, canto III, l. 9.

15. Friedrich Wilhelm Nietzsche (1844-1900) was a German philosopher whose guiding principle was the "will to power." He rejected Christian virtues and democratic ideals as being contrary to the "will to power."

16. Albert Camus (1913-1960) was a French existentialist writer of novels, dramas and essays. Much of his work reflected a view of human life as basically futile and meaningless.

17. Ernest Hemingway took his own life on July 2, 1961 in Ketchum, Idaho, where he had lived since 1958.

18. The Scopes Trial—dubbed the "monkey trial" in the press—took place in Dayton, Tennessee, in 1925 and involved the prosecution of John T. Scopes, a high school biology teacher. Scopes was accused of violating

the Butler Act, a Tennessee law that forbade teaching the theory of evolution in public schools. Clarence Darrow, then a leading criminal lawyer, defended Scopes while William Jennings Bryan, a former U.S. secretary of state, argued for the prosecution.

Scopes was convicted and fined, but the state supreme court later reversed the decision on a technicality. The Butler Act remained a law in Tennessee until 1967.

19. Russian author Fedor Dostoevski (1821-1881) was regarded, along with Tolstoi, as a master of the psychological novel. Among his many works are *Crime and Punishment* and *The Brothers Karamazov*. His writing evidenced a sympathy for human suffering and an ability to find some goodness in even the most hopeless of humans.

20. Jean-Paul Sartre (1905-1980), a noted French philosopher, novelist and dramatist, was perhaps most famous for his espousal of existentialism, the view that the individual "is alone, abandoned on earth in the midst of his infinite responsibilities without help, with no other aim than the one he sets himself, with no other destiny than the one he forges for himself on this earth" (*Being and Nothingness*, 1943).

21. *Stronger Than Steel: The Wayne Alderson Story* by R. C. Sproul (Harper & Row, Publishers, 1980) is the story of "a coal miner's son who became a corporate executive, a soldier who became a peacemaker, a Christian idealist who lives as a hard-core realist, and the founder of the widespread Value of the Person movement to reestablish labor/management relations on a positive basis" (Cover 4).

22. Masada is the mountaintop fortress, now in ruins, some 30 miles southeast of Jerusalem where some.1,000 Jewish Zealots made their last stand against Roman rule, following the destruction of Jerusalem and the Temple in A.D. 70 by Roman forces under the general Titus. When Masada could no longer hold out against the Romans, the Zealots under Eleazar ben Jair committed mass suicide to avoid having to surrender.

23. Warsaw, Poland's capital city, fell to Hitler's invading forces on September 27, 1939 and was occupied by them until January 1945. During the Nazi occupation of the city, 500,000 Jewish residents of Warsaw were forced into a walled ghetto within the city of less than one square mile. Within four months in 1942, 300,000 of the ghetto inhabitants were removed to concentration camps and killed. Then in April 1943, German troops attacked the ghetto and killed the remaining Jews who resisted bravely for three weeks before succumbing to overwhelming force.

24. A longtime member of the Nazi secret police, (Karl) Adolf Eichmann (1906-1962) was the Gestapo official charged by Hitler with "the final solution of the Jewish problem." In that capacity, he presided over the extermination of millions of Jews in German-occupied Europe.

Eichmann disappeared at the end of World War II. Then in 1960, Israeli agents tracked him down in Argentina, kidnapped him and brought him to Israel. Publicly tried in Jerusalem for crimes against humanity, he was subsequently convicted and hanged.

25. "Harold Abrahams' obsession with winning was strongly influenced by his status as the son of a German Jew, forced to battle prejudice in an English society that treated him as an alien. His running triumphs were intended to enforce his acceptance as a native son, the equal of anybody....

"Harold lived on into old age. By the time he died in 1978, he was a leading sports writer and broadcaster and the Elder Statesman of British athletics, more established in society than he had ever imagined he would be when he first started out at Cambridge." W. J. Weatherby, *Chariots of Fire* (New York: Dell Publishing Co., Inc., Quicksilver Books, Inc., 1981), pp. 16, 174.

Chapter 4

1. Elizabeth Barrett Browning (1806-1861), *Sonnets from the Portuguese*, no. 43.

2. Manichaeans were disciples of the Persian religious leader, Mani (c. A.D. 216-276), who believed himself to be last of a line of prophets that included Zoroaster, Buddha and Jesus. He claimed the revelations of his predecessors were only partial and were consummated in his own teachings.

Mani taught that the universe was divided into two ever-contending realms of good and evil. The good was the realm of Light (spirit) ruled by God and the evil was the realm of Darkness (matter), ruled by Satan—and the two are engaged in a never-ending struggle. The human body is material and, therefore, also evil. The body imprisons the soul which is spiritual and which can be redeemed only through knowledge of the realm of Light revealed by that succession of prophets who culminated in Mani.

The more spiritually perfect Manichaeans, called the elect, were ascetic in the extreme, practicing strict celibacy, vegetarianism and abstinence from wine. Interestingly, they also abstained from labor, confining themselves to preaching.

The less spiritually perfect Manichaeans, called auditors, observed weekly fasts and served the elect. They were permitted to marry, but were discouraged from procreating. Their hope was to be reborn as the elect.

Eventually, Zoroastrian leaders convinced the Persian emperor Bahram I to arrest Mani as a heretic who then either died in confinement or was executed.

For nine years prior to his conversion, St. Augustine was a Manichaean.

Chapter 6

1. Because his principles of medical science became the foundation of medical theory developed in the 1800s, the Greek physician Hippocrates (c.

460-377 B.C.) is universally regarded as the father of modern medicine and author of "The Physician's Oath." At one time, all graduating medical students took the Hippocratic oath, which reads in part:

"I swear...that I will carry out, according to my ability and judgment, this oath and this indenture....

"I will use treatment to help the sick according to my ability and judgment, but never with a view to injury and wrongdoing. Neither will I administer a poison to anybody when asked to do so, nor will I suggest such a course. Similarly, I will not give to a woman a pessary to cause abortion.

"I will keep pure and holy both my life and my art....

"In whatsoever houses I enter, I will enter to help the sick, and I will abstain from all intentional wrongdoing and harm, especially from abusing the bodies of man or woman, bond or free.

"And whatsoever I shall see or hear in the course of my profession in my intercourse with men, if it be what should not be published abroad, I will never divulge, holding such things to be holy secrets.

"Now if I carry out this oath, and break it not, may I gain forever reputation among all men for my life and for my art."

Chapter 7

1. *The World Almanac and Book of Facts 1991* (New York: Pharos Books, World Almanac, 1990), p. 850.
2. Norman Rockwell (1894-1978) was an American painter and illustrator best known as an illustrator of magazine covers for such publications as the *Saturday Evening Post,* the *Ladies' Home Journal* and *Look.* He was much beloved for his folksy, often humorous portrayals of scenes from everyday life. His work was noted for fine attention to detail and for almost photographic realism. Rockwell also painted the famous series of murals entitled *The Four Freedoms.*
3. A recent case in point: *"Morgan Wins $540,000 in Suit Over Assault by Police Officer."*

"A federal jury...awarded $540,000 to former major league baseball player Joe Morgan after determining that the Hall of Fame member was illegally detained and roughed up by a Los Angeles police officer who had mistaken Morgan for a drug carrier.

"The jurors deliberated for only 2 1/2 hours before siding with Morgan against the city of Los Angeles and Los Angeles Police Department narcotics Detective Clayton Searle, who was accused of violating Morgan's civil rights during their 1988 confrontation at Los Angeles International Airport....

"Morgan said that despite his efforts to identify himself, the narcotics officer suddenly grabbed him around the neck, hurled him to the floor, handcuffed him before a crowd of onlookers and dragged him to a small room for questioning....

"...some jurors said they believe Morgan was singled out because he is black and that he was victimized by an overzealous Searle.

"'We wanted to send a message to City Hall that police cannot act uncontrollably,' said juror Gene Dempsey, 38, of Buena Park....

"As he left the courthouse to fly back to his Oakland-area home, Morgan said he was relieved his legal ordeal was over. 'This is one of the toughest things I've ever had to do, but what he did to me may have happened to other people as well,' he said."

Los Angeles Times, February 15, 1991, p. B6.

Chapter 8

1. In a Presbyterian Church, the session is the governing body of the congregation and consists of those elders—teaching elders and ruling elders—in active service.

2. Born in Ireland, Gilbert Tennent (1703-1764), like his father before him, was a Presbyterian minister. His family immigrated to North American in 1718, and he became a leading figure in the Great Awakening revival movement that swept the American colonies during the 1740s.

   Tennent delivered his sermon, "The Danger of Unconverted Ministry" in 1740 during the time that he was a pastor in New Brunswick in the colony of New Jersey. In this sermon, he was critical of other conservative ministers who resisted the revivalist fervor of the Great Awakening because they feared it would prove harmful to established churches. The result was a schism within the Presbyterian Church which divided into "Old Side" and "New Side" factions. Tennent led the "New Siders." But in 1758, he was able to reunite and reconcile the two factions once again.

   From 1743 until his death in 1764, Tennent ministered in Philadelphia.

3. Used by permission of Mr. M. Stanton Evans.

4. On this point, the Rev. Dr. Richard C. Halverson, chaplain of the United States Senate, has written:

   "An interesting and frustrating aspect of the church/state debate has been the confusion of a comment by Thomas Jefferson made to the Baptists of Danbury, Connecticut, in 1802...: 'Believing that religion is a matter which lies solely between man and his God, that he owes account to none other for his faith or his worship, that the legislative powers of government reach actions only, and not opinions, I contemplate with sovereign reverence that act of the whole American people which declared that their legislature should make no law respecting an establishment of religion, or prohibiting the free exercise thereof, thus building a wall of separation between Church and State.'..."

   When one refers to the first amendment today, immediately Thomas Jefferson's statement comes to mind and is often, if not always, equated with the first amendment. On the basis of this interpretation we are being told over and over again that the Church has no business being involved in government or in the political process or in the influencing of public policy, which to me seems as far removed from what was in the minds of our founding fathers, including Thomas Jefferson, as is possible.

"'Congress shall make no law respect an establishment of religions, or prohibiting the free exercise thereof....' Those two clauses compose what the first amendment has to say about religion and government. If words mean anything what our founding fathers were intending was that government under no circumstances should give preferential treatment to any particular religious group, and, secondly, that government should in no way interfere in any person's or group's free exercise of faith, religious practice or worship.

"Not a word of those two clauses in the first amendment separates the Church from the state."

Richard C. Halverson, *We the People* (Ventura, CA: Regal Books, 1987), pp. 57,58,60. Used by permission.

Chapter 9

1. Joseph Raymond McCarthy (1908-57) represented Wisconsin in the U. S. Senate from 1946 until his death in 1957. In the early 1950s, as chairman of a Senate subcommittee on investigations, he alleged that various governmental departments and agencies from the State Department to the U. S. Army were infiltrated by communists and concealing those guilty of subversive activities.

   McCarthy was eventually accused of misusing his office through pressure tactics and other abuses of power. He was cleared of the various charges against him but was censured by the Senate for his investigatory methods and victimization of various individuals and bodies. Though subsequently discredited, he remained in the Senate for the remainder of his life. And ever since, the term "McCarthyism" has been applied to any sort of personal attack on individuals involving indiscriminate allegations and unsubstantiated charges.

2. J(ohn) Edgar Hoover (1895-1972) served as director of the Federal Bureau of Investigation for 48 years, from 1924 until his death. He served under every president from Calvin Coolidge to Richard Nixon.

3. The blockade of Berlin, located 100 miles inside the then German Democratic Republic (East Germany), was imposed by Soviet authorities in June 1948. All access to the city by land and water was halted. Western powers kept the city functioning by means of a massive airlift that continued until the blockade ended on May 12, 1949.

4. The Korean War began on June 25, 1950 when North Korean forces crossed the 38th parallel and invaded South Korea. U.S. and UN forces came to the aid of South Korea, and Communist China entered on the side

of North Korea. The war ended with a cease-fire in July 1953 with Korea remaining divided at the 38th parallel.

5. Afghanistan was once a kingdom, ruled by a monarchy until 1973 when a coup brought in a military government and the declaration of a republic. A second coup in 1978 brought in a pro-Soviet government that concluded an economic and military treaty with the USSR. In December 1979 the USSR began a massive movement of military personnel and materiel into Afghanistan that resulted in a Soviet-engineered coup on December 27 and the installation of a puppet government.

A nine-year guerrilla war began as Afghanistani freedom fighters rebelled against the occupation of their country by Soviet troops. The United Nations mediated an agreement signed on April 14, 1988 that provided for the withrawal of Soviet forces from Afghanistan. The withdrawal was completed on February 15, 1989, but a state of civil war continues as freedom fighters still work to dislodge the Communist government left in place by the USSR after its departure.

6. The Solidarity crisis in Poland began in 1980 following a protracted period of labor unrest that tied up the country. On August 30, 1980, in an effort to normalize matters, the government granted 21 concessions to the striking workers of the Lenin Shipyard in Gdansk. Among these concessions were the right to form independent labor unions and the right to strike, rights previously unknown in the Soviet bloc. Within a year, 9.5 million workers had joined the new independent trade union Solidarity.

On December 12, 1981, Solidarity leaders, among them Lech Walesa, proposed a nationwide referendum on establishing a non-Communist government, if the present government failed to agree to further demands such as free and democratic elections and access to the mass media. The government, fearing Soviet intervention, imposed martial law on December 13, and Lech Walesa and other Solidarity leaders were arrested.

Finally, in April 5, 1989, the government and opposition factions reached an accord that allowed for the first free elections in over 40 years. Solidarity candidates swept the election, and on August 19, Poland's first non-Communist prime minister took office. Lech Walesa himself became president of Poland after winning election for that office on December 9, 1990.

7. *The World Almanac and Book of Facts 1991* (New York: Pharos Books, World Almanac, 1990), p. 40.

8. Ibid., p. 37.

9. Ibid., p. 35.

10. Karl Marx, "Introduction," *Critique of the Hegelian Philosophy of Right* (1844).

The source of these population figures are the U.S. Bureau of the Census published in *The World Almanac and Book of Facts 1991* (New York: Pharos Books, World Almanac, 1990), p. 773.

12. "Gulag is an acronym for the dread Central Corrective Labor Camp Administration. To Solzhenitsyn, the title [*The Gulag Archipelago*] suggests that the territory of the USSR was dotted with myriad islands of concentration camps—an archipelago that was 'psychologically fused into a continent inhabited by prisoners.'" *Time*, Vol. 103, No. 1 (January 7, 1974), p. 49, footnote.

13. A reflection of this viewpoint appeared in a recent issue of *World* magazine, a publication intended "to help Christians apply the Bible to their understanding of and response to everyday current events," when a reader took the editors to task for never publishing a critique or "at least a brief expose now and then" of capitalism. This writer stated that "self-interest is the driving force behind capitalism" and expressed surprise "to find so many Christians so devoted to an economic system which is driven by greed." To buttress his case, he quoted the contemporary Catholic scholar, Michael Novak, who has stated, among other things: "At the heart of Christianity, according to Leon Bloy, lies the sinner. At the heart of capitalist creativity lies self-interest."

    The editor, Joel Belz, replied, "People are thought to be arrogant who assert that God was the original capitalist. But such caution diminishes God's glory....The wellspring of the capitalist dynamic should be seen as entirely positive and reflective of the highest kind of Godliness....Self-interest becomes a good thing when it coincides with God's interest. That is what redemption is all about—turning us around so that we want the same things he wants. When a capitalist comes to want the same things God wants, there's no longer anything wrong with his self-interest!" *World*, Vol. 3, No. 35 (February 18, 1989), pp. 2-3.

    And the debate goes on.

14. "Col." Edwin L. Drake (1819-1880) is credited with having conceived the idea of drilling for oil. Using a primitive rig that he built himself, he began drilling for oil at Titusville near Oil Creek in Pennsylvania's Venango County, some 75 miles north of Pittsburgh. On August 27, 1859, having reached a depth of less than 70 feet, Drake struck a reservoir of oil, making his pioneer effort the first commercial oil well in the world.

    Oil City at the mouth of Oil Creek on the Allegheny River was founded the next year. In the first decade after Drake struck oil, 17 million barrels from his well were shipped from Oil City to Pittsburgh.

    Drake's success was the beginning of the modern petroleum industry.

15. Thomas Alva Edison's first successful incandescent lamp was tested in his laboratory at Menlo Park, New Jersey, on October 21, 1879. Unlike his previous lamps which had burned out quickly, this one burned for more than 40 hours.

Chapter 10

1. At the time of World War I, the Siegfried Line was a part of the old Hin-

denberg Line that ran along Germany's boundary with France and which was captured by Allied forces on October 5, 1918. Though eventually destroyed, the Siegfried Line—a chain of steel forts, concrete tank barriers, pillboxes, trenches and barbed wire entanglements—was rebuilt by Adolph Hitler in 1938. It ran directly opposite the Maginot Line, a similar defense system erected by France against any possible invasion by Nazi Germany. Both countries claimed their respective fortified defense lines were impenetrable against armored assault.

In 1940, German troops did break through and cross the Maginot Line into France. Allied Forces, in turn, succeeded in breaking through the Seigfried Line many times during World War II and eventually destroyed it. In one of those operations, Wayne Alderson's Seventh Regiment assaulted and broke through the Siegfried Line in March 1945, just south of the German town of Zweibrucken. Wayne's Company B led the way, making him, as point man, the first man from the Third Division to cross into Germany. But in that action, Wayne was severely injured by a grenade, and his best buddy, Charles "Red" Preston, was killed while trying to rescue Alderson.

2. John Emerich Edward Dalberg-Acton or Lord Acton (1832-1902) wrote these words in a letter to Bishop Mandell Creighton, April 5, 1887.

3. A reference to a statement made in a speech given at the Minnesota State Fair on September 2, 1901 by President Theodore Roosevelt (1858-1919) in which he said, "There is a homely adage which runs, 'Speak softly and carry a big stick; you will go far.' If the American nation will speak softly and yet build and keep at a pitch of the highest training a thoroughly efficient navy, the Monroe Doctrine will go far."

4. *Miracle of Pittron* is available from Value of the Person, 52 Dutch Lane, Pittsburgh, Pennsylvania 15236, (412) 562-9070.